The Life, Times & Music® Series

The Life, Times & Music® Series

Martin Huxley

FRIEDMAN/FAIRFAX
P U B L I S H E R S

A FRIEDMAN/FAIRFAX BOOK

© 1995 by Friedman/Fairfax Publishers

ISBN 1-56799-227-7

Editor: Stephen Slaybaugh
Art Director: Jeff Batzli
Design: Elan Studio
Cover Design: Zemsky Design
Photography Editor: Emilya Naymark
Production Manager: Jeanne E. Kaufman

Grateful acknowledgment is given to authors, publishers, and photographers for permission to reprint material. Every effort has been made to determine copyright owners of photographs and illustrations. In the case of any omissions, the publishers will be pleased to make suitable acknowledgments in future editions.

Printed in the United States of America
by Quebecor Printing Semline, Inc.

For bulk purchases and special sales, please contact:
Friedman/Fairfax Publishers
Attention: Sales Department
15 West 26 Street
New York, NY 10010
(212) 685-6610 FAX (212) 685-1307

website: *http: //www.webcom.com/~friedman*

CONTENTS

Introduction..........6

Jimi Hendrix..........12

The Grateful Dead..........16

Jefferson Airplane..........20

Quicksilver Messenger Service..........24

The Byrds..........27

Love..........30

The Doors..........32

Spirit..........36

Iron Butterfly..........39

Steppenwolf..........41

The Chambers Brothers..........44

The Strawberry Alarm Clock..........45

The 13th Floor Elevators..........46

Donovan..........50

Traffic..........52

Pink Floyd..........55

Conclusion..........59

Suggested Reading..........60

Suggested Listening..........60

Index..........61

INTRODUCTION

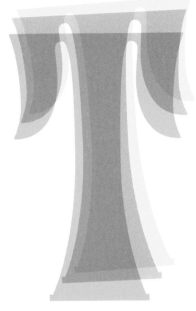

o get really high is to forget yourself. And to forget yourself is to see everything else. And to see everything else is to become an understanding molecule in evolution, a conscious tool of the universe.

—Jerry Garcia

The word *psychedelic*—a scientific term literally meaning "mind-expanding"—was originally used in connection with the hallucinogenic drugs that the U.S. government began experimenting with in the 1950s. In the second half of the 1960s, however, the term came to represent a newly emerging underground culture and the music that provided its soundtrack.

Psychedelic rock was originally designated as such due to the influence of LSD and other psychedelic substances in its creation, and for the music's propensity for conveying the experience of an acid trip. But not all psychedelic music is drug-influenced, and not all drug-influenced music is psychedelic. The real spirit of psychedelia lies in the impulse to view the universe through an altered

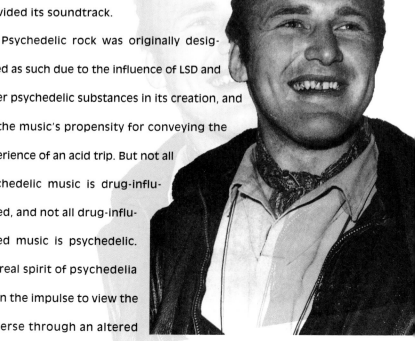

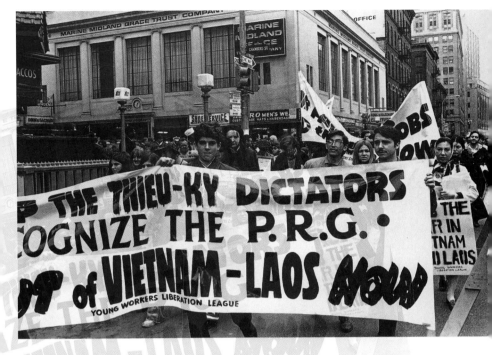

Opposite: Ken Kesey, author of *One Flew Over the Cuckoo's Nest*, and his Merry Pranksters were key instigators of the psychedelic movement and staged Acid Tests in such cities as San Jose and Los Angeles. He is shown here after being arrested in 1966 by FBI agents for marijuana possession—a felony at the time. Above: Protesters march in a Vietnam War moratorium demonstation in Manhattan on April 15, 1970.

perspective—though not necessarily chemically—in the course of a quest for cosmic enlightenment and/or a good time.

Lysergic acid diethylamide, more commonly known by its chemical abbreviation LSD, was first introduced to the world through U.S. government experiments in the 1950s. Its first high-profile champions were Harvard professor Timothy Leary (b. 1920), who'd been fired for his LSD experiments, and writer Ken Kesey (b. 1935), who in 1965 had been administered doses of government-issued acid, mescaline, and psilocybin as a volunteer in a Stanford University research project. Kesey, with his aptly named band of followers, the Merry Pranksters, subsequently built a celebratory lifestyle around the still-legal drug, journeying through California ingesting LSD-laced Kool-Aid—an odyssey chronicled in Tom Wolfe's seminal book *The Electric Kool-Aid Acid Test*.

Although such early LSD enthusiasts as San Francisco's Grateful Dead and Texas's 13th Floor Elevators had been making deeply acid-influenced

music since 1965, the pivotal year for the new, psychedelicized counterculture was 1967. As a deeply unpopular war raged in Vietnam, popular music increasingly reflected the mood of protest, rebellion, and reflectiveness among America's youth. With the increasingly widespread availability of marijuana and psychedelic drugs, hippie communities sprang up across the country, invariably centered around vital musical scenes.

Psychedelic ballrooms such as the Fillmore and the Avalon Ballroom in San Francisco, the Electric Circus and the Fillmore East in New York, the Cheetah in Los Angeles, the Aragon in Chicago, the Tea Party in Boston, and the Grande Ballroom in Detroit played host to multi-act bills that were as much tribal

Top: Transplanted Texan Janis Joplin was the San Francisco scene's most distinctive voice as well as one of its most charismatic personalities. Above: The heart of the sixties' psychedelic movement, the Haight-Ashbury district was always filled with people just "hanging out."

Bay Area rock impresario Bill Graham, born Wolfgang Grajonca in Poland, escaped from the Nazis as a child. He was known for the tenacity he brought to his work as the San Francisco scene's most influential concert promoter.

bonding celebrations as they were concerts, invariably advertised with flamboyant posters and accompanied by hyperkinetic light shows that heightened psychedelia's multimedia, multitextural, and multisensoral experience.

The psychedelic movement's unquestioned epicenter was San Francisco's run-down Haight-Ashbury district, which had years earlier become host to a bohemian community whose numbers swelled with an ever-growing influx of societal dropouts, disaffected UC Berkeley students, and aspiring writers, artists, and musicians. The Bay Area's tradition of boho culture and radical politics, as well as its mild climate and bucolic natural beauty, made it a natural atmosphere in which bands like the Charlatans, the Grateful Dead, Jefferson Airplane, Quicksilver Messenger Service, Country Joe and the Fish, and Big Brother and the Holding Company (featuring Texas transplant Janis Joplin) could thrive. The Bay Area was also the home base of affluent LSD chemist Owsley, a.k.a. Augustus Owsley Stanley III, who manufactured a variety of high-quality hallucinogens that he often distributed free of charge at countercultural public events.

Landmark events in the development of the San Francisco scene included the three-day Trips Festival, a multimedia bash instigated by Kesey and his Merry Pranksters and produced by budding local rock promoter Bill Graham (b. 1931). The Festival, featuring virtually every notable local band, drew ten thousand revelers in January 1966. Soon after, Graham and the scene's other notable promoter, Chet Helms, began taking turns producing shows at the Fillmore on alternate weekends; Helms later moved to the Avalon, and Graham took over the Fillmore full-time. And on January 14, 1967, the Grateful Dead, Jefferson Airplane, Quicksilver Messenger Service, and Country Joe and the Fish all performed at the first Human Be-In, which attracted twenty thousand people to Golden Gate Park.

By the summer of 1967, media coverage of the "Summer of Love" was inescapable. The mainstream music industry discovered the new rock and recognized its nascent commercial potential—even if most industry leaders couldn't relate to the music's sociopolitical implications. Though psychedelia sporadically seeped into the mainstream pop charts through the hit singles of the Airplane, the Doors, and Scottish Day-Glo troubadour Donovan (not to mention such flukes as "Journey to the Center of the Mind" by Detroit garage-rockers the Amboy Dukes, featuring future heavy metal star Ted Nugent), it seems unlikely that the music could have seriously penetrated the American consciousness without the almost accidental advent of progressive free-form FM radio stations.

With AM pop-music formats growing increasingly restrictive in the mid-sixties, FM rock was spawned after the Federal Communications Commission (not known before or since as a friend to the counterculture) ruled that its licensees broadcasting on both bands could not simply duplicate their AM broadcasts over the FM band, as was common practice at the time. In the summer of 1965, New York's WOR-FM—which had been duplicating its AM counterpart's talk shows—switched to a free-form rock format. The

The most influential songwriter of the sixties, Bob Dylan, whose songs were marked by complex, sardonic wordplay, opened new doors of expression for a generation of would-be troubadours.

new WOR-FM, under the direction of former Top 40 deejay and self-proclaimed "fifth Beatle" Murray the K, hit the air with a revolutionary mix of longer album cuts, soft-spoken deejays, and extended sets uninterrupted by ads or station jingles. He had instantly created a medium for more adventurous rock music, and in turn made new, more challenging (and previously radio-unfriendly) rock

The Beatles' groundbreaking *Sgt. Pepper's Lonely Hearts Club Band* demonstrated the dynamics of studio recording and initiated a wave of "experimental" albums.

acts more commercially viable—and it wasn't long before the progressive-rock format had been adopted by stations across the country.

Elsewhere, psychedelia became an essential element in the work of rock's most influential creators. Observers of Bob Dylan (b. 1941) had long speculated about the influence of psychedelics on the complex linguistics of his lyrics. Dylan himself was typically elusive in discussing the topic: "I wouldn't advise anybody to use drugs, certainly not the hard drugs," he said in 1966. "But opium and hash and pot—now, those things aren't drugs; they just bend your mind a little. I think everybody's mind should be bent every once in a while." Meanwhile, the Beatles' psychedelic experiments were a key contributor to their masterwork, *Sgt. Pepper's Lonely Hearts Club Band*. Beach Boys mastermind Brian Wilson's chemical dabblings were reflected in his innovative expansions of the pop-song format on the classic album *Pet Sounds* and the legendary unreleased opus *Smile*. The Rolling Stones temporarily deserted their hard-edged trademark style for the hallucinatory visions of *Their Satanic Majesties Request*. Even Animals leader Eric Burdon, previously one of the British Invasion's scrappiest blues wailers, jumped headfirst into psychedelia, moving to San Francisco and abandoning his band's no-frills style in favor of an awkward cosmic-voyager persona.

Although psychedelia more or less died out as a genre in the early 1970s, it has created rock and roll ripples that continue to spread. Some of the bands that popularized the sound were (or came to be) major acts, while others were, perhaps undeservedly, lesser known, such as Love and Spirit. All of them, however, shared a certain mind-bending (or mind-bent) outlook, as well as a desire to share that attitude—or its fruit—with the rock and roll public.

JIMI HENDRIX

If any one musician personified the psychedelic era's ideals of sonic innovation and free-spirited iconoclasm, it was Jimi Hendrix (1942–1970). In a four-year recording career whose brevity is belied by its far-reaching influence, Hendrix single-handedly redefined the parameters of rock guitar playing, while effortlessly embodying the fusion of black and white musical styles that formed the basis of rock 'n' roll. With one foot planted firmly in the earthy emotionality of the blues and the other in the liberating spirit of jazz, Hendrix built an audaciously personal synthesis of styles that has never been matched for its sheer intensity and expressiveness.

The Aquarian Age's essential axe hero, Jimi Hendrix combined unparalleled instrumental and compositional chops with an effortless personal charisma.

Hendrix was ahead of his time in several crucial respects. While he was hardly the first guitarist to experiment with feedback and distortion, he was the first to fully integrate those experiments into a personalized musical vocabulary. If Hendrix's technique was innovative and individual, his songwriting was unique in its combination of cosmic mysticism and earthy sensuality. And the fact that he was a black man working in the mostly white field of sixties rock only served to bolster Hendrix's status as a mythic figure.

As a middle-class teenager growing up in Seattle, Hendrix taught himself guitar by playing along with records by blues masters Muddy Waters and B.B. King and early rockers Eddie Cochran and Chuck Berry. After a stint in the army ended with a discharge due to injuries sustained while parachuting, Hendrix found work as a hired gun on the club circuit under the pseudonym Jimmy James, backing such greats as Little Richard, Wilson Pickett, Jackie Wilson, and Ike and Tina Turner. Relocating to New York in 1964, Hendrix hit the Greenwich Village club scene, where he played with the likes of King Curtis, the Isley Brothers, white blues revivalist John Paul Hammond, and soul singer Curtis Knight. Though his dissatisfaction with his own singing voice initially kept him from striking out on his own, Hendrix—inspired by Bob Dylan's success—eventually launched his own combo, Jimmy James and the Blue Flames.

In the autumn of 1966, he was spotted by Animals bassist Chas Chandler, who took him to London and hooked him up with an English rhythm section (bassist Noel Redding [b. 1945] and drummer Mitch Mitchell [b. 1947]) to form the Jimi

Hendrix Experience. Chandler dressed the trio in flamboyant Carnaby Street threads and encouraged Hendrix to play up his own personal outrageousness and musical flamboyance—a direction that would come to haunt the guitarist in the near future, but which at the time served as a helpful attention-getter.

With the trio's debut single, "Hey Joe," reaching number six on the U.K. charts, Hendrix and his new bandmates quickly became the toast of London's pop aristocracy. By the summer of 1967, the American rock scene was abuzz with word of the guitarist's flashy performance style and incendiary instrumental technique. The band's U.S. debut at the Monterey Pop Festival in June 1967 (reportedly at the instigation of Paul McCartney) proved to be a brilliant coming-out party, with Hendrix picking with his teeth, playing behind his back, humping his amp, and setting fire to his guitar—an act that felt less like an expression of mindless destruction than a ritual sacrifice and one that added an indelible image to rock's visual lexicon.

The Jimi Hendrix Experience's startling 1967 debut LP, *Are You Experienced?*, was a breakthrough in more ways than one, demonstrating the amazing breadth of his talents. Songs such as "Purple Haze" (as compelling a musical evocation of the acid experience as any yet created), "Manic Depression," "Fire," and "The Wind Cries Mary" combined Jimi's oddball inventiveness with lyrics that forthrightly addressed primal issues of fear, lust, and loneliness. Hendrix's blistering variations on blues and rock styles were unlike anything previously

Before moving to England to form the Jimi Hendrix Experience, Hendrix played backing guitar with many bands.

heard in rock. The album's near-instant sales success—half a million copies without the benefit of a Top 40 single, a feat virtually unheard of at the time—helped to usher in the album-rock era.

The subsequent *Axis: Bold As Love* (which balanced mind-warping blues-inspired flights alongside ethereal ballads like "Little Wing" and "Castles Made of Sand") and the tour de force double album *Electric Ladyland* (featuring the mythic "Voodoo Child," the funk-inflected "Crosstown Traffic," and a brilliant rendition of Dylan's "All Along the Watchtower") further extended Hendrix's accomplishments as a player, songwriter, and manipulator of the recording medium, and demonstrated how solidly he had integrated his influences into a singular style.

By that point, Hendrix—always more concerned with his identity as a serious musician than with his image as a rock star—had became frustrated that his talents as a player and songwriter had been overshadowed by his cosmic love-child persona. As his ambivalence toward his success grew, he renounced the flashy stage pyrotechnics and concentrated on playing music. Torn between his own desire to play more challenging music and his management's insistence on sticking with the tried and true, Hendrix became increasingly withdrawn, retreating to the solace of his newly built Greenwich Village recording studio, Electric Lady.

A combination of artistic restlessness, tension between band members, and pressure from black activists for the apolitical Hendrix to play with African-American musicians caused the Experience to splinter in early 1969. That summer, Hendrix played at the Woodstock festival with an ad hoc ensemble dubbed Electric Sky Church. Later in the year, he put together the more funk-oriented all-black trio Band of Gypsys with two old friends, bassist Billy Cox and drummer Buddy Miles (b. 1946). That lineup largely abandoned Hendrix's previous psychedelic orientation in favor of harder-edged funk and jazz variations; a recording of Band of Gypsys' debut show, at New York's Fillmore East on New Year's Eve, 1969, became that band's only album.

Despite its initial promise, Hendrix put the Band of Gypsys to rest a few months later, walking offstage in the middle of a benefit performance at New York's Madison Square Garden. After a brief attempt at reassembling the original Experience, he returned to live work backed by Cox and Mitchell, but his performance at the August 1970 Isle of Wight Festival would prove to be his last. Jimi Hendrix died on September 18, apparently as a result of accidentally suffocating on his own vomit during barbiturate intoxication.

The following year saw the release of *The Cry of Love*, a compilation of songs that were at varying points of completion at the time of Hendrix's death. That album proved to be the first in a flood of posthumous (and generally marginal) Hendrix products that would continue to saturate the market

Hendrix, perhaps rock's most influential guitarist, was left-handed but played a right-handed guitar upside down.

for years. These included openly exploitative releases of tapes from his early days as a session player as well as a series of albums approved by the Hendrix estate and overseen by producer Alan Douglas. The latter, including such now out-of-print items as *Crash Landing*, *Midnight Lightning*, and *Nine to the Universe*, were assembled from hundreds of hours' worth of informal songs and jams recorded at Electric Lady during the last year of Hendrix's life and cobbled together by Douglas, who edited various takes and added newly recorded instrumental tracks—much to the consternation of Hendrix purists.

Despite his success, Hendrix himself always expressed dissatisfaction with his own output, speaking frequently of his frustration at being unable to produce all the sounds he heard in his head. Nevertheless, his legacy continues to exercise an unmistakable influence all over the musical map.

THE GRATEFUL DEAD

The Grateful Dead's remarkable history is an epic shaggy-dog story unlike anything else in the annals of rock. When these iconoclastic musical and chemical adventurers first took their place at the center of San Francisco's bohemian community in 1965, they must have seemed decidedly unlikely candidates to become the only band of their peer group to survive three decades' worth of cultural and societal upheaval with their original personnel, musical approach, and social ideals more or less intact.

Thirty years into a "long strange trip" that shows no sign of losing momentum, the Grateful Dead is not only one of rock's most durable institutions but also one of its most profitable touring acts. Maintaining a closeness with its fans that gives new meaning to the term "cult following," the group's relationship with its hardcore followers (affectionately known as "Deadheads") often seems more like religion than show business, with a remarkably organized and resourceful international network of fans having built a virtual lifestyle around the band. "Our audience is like people who like licorice," guitarist-frontman Jerry Garcia (b. 1942–1995) once stated. "Not everybody likes licorice, but the people who like licorice really like licorice."

One of the many respects in which the Dead—with its longstanding core consisting of guitarists Garcia and Bob Weir (b. 1947), bassist Phil Lesh (b. 1940),

The Grateful Dead's Jerry Garcia, a.k.a. "Captain Trips," shown here in 1970, died on August 9, 1995 at a drug- and alcohol-rehabilitation center in Northern California. Garcia's improvisational guitar textures were among the Dead's most beloved features.

and drummers Mickey Hart (b. 1950) and Bill Kreutzmann (b. 1946)—differ from virtually every other major rock act is that the group's relationship with its fans is based largely on live performance. Indeed, the group's dozen or so studio albums generally seem more like footnotes than landmarks. The Dead's no-two-alike marathon concerts are mass bonding rituals that inspire the most committed Deadheads to follow the band's tours from city to city and to amass huge collections of live concert recordings (the band does not discourage fans from recording live shows).

At early Grateful Dead shows, it was hard to tell who ingested more illicit chemicals, the audience or the band.

The Grateful Dead's intimate rapport with its audience can be traced back to the communal atmosphere that surrounded the ensemble's early days, when this motley assemblage of former folk, blues, bluegrass, and jug-band musicians shared a house in the Haight-Ashbury district of San Francisco. By the time the Warlocks changed their name to the Grateful Dead in November 1965, they had already discovered LSD through an alliance with Ken Kesey and his Merry Pranksters: the group received its first major exposure as the house band at Kesey's now-legendary Acid Tests, a series of public parties–cum–media events. Another key figure in the band's early days was famed LSD chemist Owsley, who financed the band and later supervised the building of its high-tech concert sound system.

In January 1966, the Dead—whose live sets already featured complex, wildly eclectic improvisational tangents—were a prominent attraction of the three-day Trips Festival, which attracted an audience of ten thousand and marked Bill Graham's coming-out as the scene's most prominent promoter. By the time the "Summer of Love" arrived in 1967, the band was a fixture at such local venues as the Fillmore, the Avalon, and the Carousel; they topped off the summer with an attention-getting set at the Monterey Pop Festival.

After recording a single for the local Scorpio label and a brief, unproductive liaison with MGM, the Dead signed with Warner Bros. in 1967 and re-

Above: The Dead in a late-seventies incarnation, including Donna (second from left) and Keith Godchaux (right), who were with the band from 1973 to 1979. Opposite: Bob Weir's rhythm-guitar strumming provided a structure for Garcia's long, drifting solos to glide over.

leased a self-titled debut album filled with uncharacteristically fast-tempoed three-minute songs. The more elaborate *Anthem of the Sun* and *Aoxomoxoa*, which introduced the popular live numbers "St. Stephen" and "China Cat Sunflower," translated the Dead's experimental heart into the recording medium, employing extended compositions, real-time improvisations, and unconventional recording techniques. The albums also left the band heavily in debt to Warner Bros.

The Grateful Dead ushered in the 1970s with three of their most popular releases, the in-concert *Live/Dead* (1969) and the studio efforts *Workingman's Dead* (1970) and *American Beauty* (1970). The 1970 releases found these quintessential jam-meisters taking another unexpected turn, delivering immaculately crafted country-rock tunes like "Uncle John's Band," "Truckin'," "Casey Jones," "Ripple," and "Box of Rain." The band fulfilled its commitment to Warner Bros. with a pair of live albums, *Grateful Dead Live* (1971) (better known to fans as "Skull and Roses") and *Europe '72*, before launching their own Grateful Dead label, which released *Wake of the Flood* (1973), *From the Mars Hotel* (1974), *Blues for Allah* (1975), and the live *Steal Your Face* (1976), as well as outside projects by various band members. In 1973 original keyboardist Ron "Pigpen" McKernan (b. 1945)

died from the ravages of his alcoholism; ominously, subsequent replacements Keith Godchaux (1948–1980) and Brent Mydland (1953–1990) would suffer similarly premature demises.

A move to Clive Davis's new Arista label resulted in the well-crafted but largely unsatisfying studio albums *Terrapin Station* (1977), *Shakedown Street* (1978), and *Go to Heaven* (1980) before the band returned to its old pattern with live albums like *Reckoning* (1981) and *Dead Set* (1981). In 1978, the Dead added to its cosmic credentials by playing three much-publicized concerts at the foot of Egypt's Great Pyramid.

During the first half of the eighties, though as popular a live act as ever, the Dead seemed to fall into the doldrums, with long-term observers detecting a growing tendency to fall back on established patterns rather than seeking new musical challenges. In 1985, Garcia was arrested for heroin possession and admitted to a hard-drug habit. The next year, he lapsed into a potentially fatal diabetic coma. He recovered, and the Dead emerged from the ordeal with a new sense of purpose.

Perhaps the most unexpected evidence of the Grateful Dead's belated second wind arrived in 1987 with the band's first-ever Top Ten album *In the Dark,* which contained their first-ever Top 40 single, "Touch of Grey." Along with the new platinum-level success came a new flood of attention from mainstream media outlets, generally paying admiring tribute to the band's survivor status. Another visible indicator of the Dead's new acceptance was the 1991 tribute album *Deadicated,* which features such diverse performers as Elvis Costello, Lyle Lovett, Suzanne Vega, and Midnight Oil interpreting the band's compositions.

The 1967-model Jefferson Airplane—clockwise from top left—Jack Casady, Grace Slick, Marty Balin, Spencer Dryden, Paul Kantner, and Jorma Kaukonen—garnered a strong reputation with a stellar performance at the Monterey Pop Festival.

JEFFERSON AIRPLANE

If the Grateful Dead epitomized the hippie movement's stubborn iconoclasm, then their San Francisco contemporary Jefferson Airplane demonstrated how counterculture rock could jibe comfortably with mainstream tastes. Though the Airplane was prominent in the emerging Haight-Ashbury community and adhered strongly to the hippie tribal ethic, it was also the first San Francisco group to land a record deal and the first to achieve commercial acceptance. The band's success can be attributed to its members' broad range of songwriting and performing abilities; that same surplus of talent ultimately contributed to the tensions that caused the Airplane to splinter.

Like many of its contemporaries, the band started as a group of folkies swayed by electric rock's potential for broader communication. Marty Balin (b. 1942) and Paul Kantner (b. 1942) launched the Airplane in 1965 with singer Signe Toly Anderson (b. 1941), guitarist Jorma Kaukonen (b. 1940), drummer Alexander "Skip" Spence, and bassist Bob Harvey, who was replaced by Jack Casady (b. 1944) before the band played its first major show at Balin's Matrix Club that August. By the end of the year, the Airplane signed with RCA, and an album of well-crafted but overly polite folk-rock, *Jefferson Airplane Takes Off*, followed in September 1966.

Just prior to the debut album's release, Anderson left to become a mother. Her replacement arrived in the person of former fashion model Grace Slick (b. 1939), previously a member of the Airplane-inspired Bay Area group the Great Society. Also out was Spence, who would soon resurface as one of Moby Grape's three singer-guitarists; replacing Spence was former jazz drummer Spencer Dryden (b. 1943).

The addition of the forceful, stentorian-voiced Slick gave the band a commanding performer who could match Balin's soaring vocal flights. Slick was prominently featured on the Airplane's 1966 sophomore effort, *Surrealistic Pillow*, for which the band employed Jerry Garcia as "spiritual advisor" to help communicate the band's ideas to the straitlaced staff producer that the label had assigned to the project. The album found the Airplane hitting its stride, melding its hippie-psychedelic leanings and a diverse array of folk, pop, and blues elements, along with an expanded lyrical sensibility that merged political idealism and biting social satire.

Surrealistic Pillow featured "Somebody to Love" and "White Rabbit," two Slick-sung tunes drawn from the Great Society's repertoire; both became Top Ten singles, despite the fact that the latter was banned by some radio stations for its unmistakable drug imagery. Balin weighed in with the rocking "Three-fifths of a Mile in 10 Seconds" and the affecting ballads "Today" and "Comin' Back to Me." *Surrealistic Pillow's* AM-radio success marked acid rock's first major incursion into the pop mainstream, simultaneously establishing Jefferson Airplane as both pop stars and underground heroes.

The band's next effort, *After Bathing at Baxter's* (1967), was as forbiddingly experimental as *Surrealistic Pillow* had been invitingly accessible. Not surprisingly, it didn't sell nearly as well as its predecessor, but the Airplane's musical and commercial fortunes rebounded with 1968's *Crown of Creation*. That album included Slick's folky fable "Lather," Kantner's sci-fi-inspired title track, and Slick's rendition of David Crosby's "Triad," a song about a ménage à trois that Crosby's then-band the Byrds had rejected. Crown was followed in 1969 by an impressive live album, *Bless Its Pointed Little Head*.

The fact that Jefferson Airplane was a featured act at both the Woodstock festival and its darker, West Coast counterpart, Altamont, was a clear indication of the band's status as counterculture standard-bearers. At the Altamont, the slightly-built Balin was knocked unconscious by a considerably larger Hell's Angel

Even as Jefferson Starship moved towards bland corporate rock, Slick remained a compelling performer.

when the singer attempted to stop the biker—a member of the private security force hired for the occasion by the Rolling Stones—from beating up an audience member.

Despite the Airplane's success, internal tensions—particularly between Balin and Slick—were beginning to affect the band's momentum. The cracks in the group's creative direction were evident in the sprawling 1969 album *Volunteers,* whose darker-hued lyrics reflected both the band's sinking morale as well as the dispiriting hard knocks that the Age of Aquarius had suffered since the Summer of Love. *Volunteers* was bookended by the bracing anthems "We Can Be Together" and "Volunteers" and featured contributions from the likes of Jerry Garcia, David Crosby, and Stephen Stills. By this point, the Airplane's contract with RCA allowed the band complete creative control, ending long-standing corporate battles over the band's use of foul language. Despite that rather significant victory, *Volunteers* would prove to be the band's last moment of greatness. Soon after, Jefferson Airplane took an extended break from touring while Slick was pregnant with her and Kantner's daughter China.

With the Airplane on hold, Kaukonen and Casady formed the blues- and folk-influenced offshoot Hot Tuna, while Kantner, Slick, Balin, and various friends worked on Kantner's elaborate concept album *Blows Against the Empire.* An ambitious science-fiction narrative with thematic ties to the Airplane's psychedelic roots, *Blows* was credited to "Paul Kantner and Jefferson Starship."

Jefferson Airplane returned to active duty with the 1971 album *Bark,* the first release on the band's new RCA-distributed Grunt label. But the album, like its follow-up, *Long John Silver,* and the live *Thirty Seconds Over Winterland,* showed the Airplane to be running on fumes. Indeed, the Kantner-Slick and Kaukonen-Casady factions seemed more interested in their side projects than the parent band, as evidenced by Kantner and Slick's 1971 effort *Sunfighter* and the pair's 1973 collaboration with ex–Quicksilver Messenger Service member David Freiberg, *Baron Von Tollbooth and the Chrome Nun.*

In early 1974, Kantner and Slick revived the name Jefferson Starship for their new full-time band, which included Freiberg, nineteen-year-old guitarist Craig Chaquico (b. 1955), fifty-five-year-old fiddler Papa John Creach (b. 1917), ex-Turtles drummer John Barbata, and Jorma Kaukonen's brother Peter on bass (soon replaced by British session man Pete Sears). Balin made a guest appearance on the band's debut album, *Dragon Fly* (1974), and joined full-time

Jefferson Airplane played many outdoor concerts like this one in New York City's Central Park in 1968.

for 1975's *Red Octopus*. The latter album went to number one, as did Balin's ballad single "Miracles," but the Starship's growing emphasis on faceless corporate rock mystified longtime fans and seemed needlessly mercenary in light of the Airplane's earlier idealism and adventurousness.

Subsequent releases like *Spitfire and Earth* maintained the Starship's platinum status, but the old internal rivalries reasserted themselves. Slick's long-standing alcohol problems caused her to quit the band in the middle of a European tour. Balin quit soon after, and Kantner regrouped with ex–Elvin Bishop vocalist Mickey Thomas for the anonymous-sounding 1979 outing *Freedom at Point Zero*. In the eighties, Slick returned, Kantner left, and Jefferson Starship shortened its name to Starship; the band continued to record soulless, mainstream fare like "We Built This City" and "Nothing's Gonna Stop Us Now." Slick left again in 1988, leaving Chaquico and Thomas at the helm.

Meanwhile, Kantner hooked up with Balin and Casady in 1986 for a one-album stint as the KBC Band. Three years later, Slick, Kantner, Balin, Kaukonen, and Casady reunited for a less-than-timely one-shot Jefferson Airplane album and tour. When last heard from, Kantner, Balin, and Casady were touring under the Jefferson Starship name again, while Thomas and Chaquico continued to perform as Starship.

QUICKSILVER MESSENGER SERVICE

Though they never achieved the household-name status of such scene-mates as the Grateful Dead and Jefferson Airplane, Quicksilver Messenger Service—one of the first of San Francisco's original hippie bands, and one of the last to score a recording contract—was the city's tightest live band, with a propensity for blues-based jamming that was never fully captured on the group's albums.

By the time their self-titled debut release appeared in 1968, Quicksilver had already been a local fixture for three years. The group originally consisted of guitarists John Cipollina (1943–1989) and Gary Duncan (b. 1946), bassist David Freiberg (b. 1938), drummer Greg Elmore (b. 1946), and harmonica player Jim Murray (who would depart when the band went pro); New York–bred singer-guitarist Dino Valenti (b. 1946) was the band's original instigator, but he had been jailed for marijuana possession before the group began gigging.

Quicksilver's formation coincided with the earliest rumblings of the Bay Area psychedelic scene, and the group quickly became local favorites, initially finding live work so plentiful that they didn't bother seeking a record deal. Their musical philosophy, according to Duncan, was "If you played a song the same way twice, it wasn't music anymore." Unlike many of their contemporaries, however, Quicksilver possessed the instrumental chops to translate that conceit into consistently compelling live performances.

Cipollina, whose stinging, slithery leads were one of the band's most identifiable features, had been playing in local rock bands since the late fifties; Duncan and Elmore had been in the semi-successful garage band the

Brogues, whose singles included the garage-rock classic "I Ain't No Miracle Worker"; and Freiberg was a young veteran of the folk scene.

The band—which eventually left San Francisco for an eighty-acre (32ha) ranch in nearby Marin County—was signed by Capitol in the wake of their successful appearance at the Monterey Pop Festival. Their self-titled debut album was released in May 1968, and *Happy Trails* followed six months later. The latter collection captured Quicksilver at its improvisational peak, with a side-long twenty-five-minute live version of Bo Diddley's "Who Do You Love," a track which itself was edited down from an even longer concert performance.

After *Happy Trails*, Duncan quit and moved to New York, where he briefly put together a band with Quicksilver founder Dino Valenti, who'd spent a year and a half behind bars following the aforementioned pot bust. In Duncan's absence, Cipollina, Freiberg, and Elmore recorded a third album, *Shady Grove*,

"Fresh Air" off of 1970's *Just For Love* was Quicksilver Messenger Service's first single to hit the U.S. charts.

Dino Valenti, shown here (second from left) with the group at the Fillmore East, returned to the band in 1970.

with ace English session man Nicky Hopkins (b. 1944) sitting in on piano; the band liked Hopkins' work so much that they invited him to stay on as a full-time member. Duncan returned in 1970 with Valenti, who ended up writing and singing most of the songs on the band's next LP, *Just for Love*. Though many of the group's old fans objected to the more song-oriented, laid-back direction, the album was a success, yielding the group's biggest single to date, Valenti's "Fresh Air." Freiberg, Cipollina, and Hopkins left after 1971's *What About Me*, whose title track became a popular protest anthem. Duncan, Valenti, and Elmore kept the band going for two more unsuccessful LPs before disbanding in 1973; two years later, Cipollina and Freiberg joined the trio for a one-album reunion.

Gary Duncan resurfaced in 1989 with a new incarnation of the band, its name now officially shortened to Quicksilver, which released an album, *Peace by Piece*, on Capitol. John Cipollina, who'd been plagued by illness for most of his life, died on May 29, 1989, at age forty-five; Duncan, Freiberg, Elmore, and Hopkins reunited for an all-star memorial show at Bill Graham's reopened Fillmore. Hopkins and Valenti died soon after. Duncan, meanwhile, has kept his version of Quicksilver together, with Freiberg rejoining during the nineties.

THE BYRDS

The Byrds were (arguably) the first and (definitely) the most prominent practitioners of the sixties folk-rock subgenre, setting in motion a movement that would generate some of the decade's most memorable music. The band's lengthy career would bring numerous personnel changes and a variety of stylistic turns—including the psychedelic period that would yield the precedent-setting classic "Eight Miles High"—but the Byrds would always maintain the sense of restless yet accessible experimentalism that first endeared them to their fans.

The Byrds was originally the brainchild of Jim (who later changed his name to Roger) McGuinn (b. 1942), a folkie who'd been struck by the idea of combining the sophisticated, message-oriented wordplay popularized by Bob Dylan with the rock electricity of the Beatles. The Chicago-born McGuinn had played guitar with the likes of Judy Collins, Chad Mitchell, Bobby Darin, and the Limelighters before his viewing of The Beatles' film *A Hard Day's Night* inspired him to buy an electric twelve-string and form the band of his dreams. He found kindred spirits in fellow folksingers Gene Clark (b. 1941) and David

The Byrds in their original and most popular incarnation—from left to right, Chris Hillman, Roger McGuinn, Gene Clark, Michael Clarke, and David Crosby—were once touted as "America's answer to the Beatles."

Crosby (b. 1941), bluegrass mandolinist Chris Hillman (b. 1942) (who quickly mastered bass guitar), and beach bum Michael Clarke (b. 1943) (who had little musical experience but looked right for the role of drummer).

The quintet formed in 1964 as the Jet Set and was briefly known as the Beefeaters before settling on the Byrds—misspelled in tribute to the Beatles. Before long, they'd received Dylan's personal endorsement and arrived, through trial and error, at a distinctive and timely style spotlighting McGuinn's and Crosby's chiming guitars and the spotless vocal harmonies of McGuinn, Clark, and Crosby. The Byrds' debut single, released in the summer of 1965, was a streamlined reworking of Dylan's "Mr. Tambourine Man" (on which McGuinn provided the trademark twelve-string and the cream of L.A.'s session musicians handled the rest of the instruments) that became a number one single. They followed it with another anthemic folk-derived hit, "Turn! Turn! Turn!," a biblical passage set to music by Pete Seeger.

In 1966 the band expanded its pursuits into more experimental—and explicitly psychedelic—territory with its third LP, *Fifth Dimension*. Along with the careening "I See You" and the tongue-in-cheek sci-fi novelty "Mr. Spaceman," the collection included the band's high-flying "space rock" epic "Eight Miles High," which featured Coltrane-influenced guitar excursions, a thunderous bass line, soaring massed vocals, and surrealistic sci-fi imagery. The song's supposedly drug-inspired lyrics got it banned from many radio stations, though the band always insisted that the words were inspired by the

airplane flight that began their disastrous tour of England the previous summer. In addition to crystallizing the Byrds' experimental leanings, "Eight Miles High" also marked cowriter Gene Clark's final contribution to the band; ironically, one of the main reasons for his departure was his intense fear of flying.

The Byrds continued to integrate psychedelic elements on the subsequent albums *Younger Than Yesterday* (1967) and *The Notorious Byrd Brothers* (1968) before making an unexpected and, at the time, radical about-face to embrace rural music traditions on 1968's *Sweetheart of the Rodeo*—the band's only album recording during Gram Parsons' brief tenure. By that point, David Crosby and Michael Clarke were long gone, and Hillman would soon follow, leaving to form the country-rock Flying Burrito Brothers with Parsons. The Byrds' next incarnation—featuring bluegrass veteran Clarence White (b. 1944) on guitar—audaciously integrated acid-rock and country elements on subsequent albums like *Dr. Byrds and Mr. Hyde, Ballad of Easy Rider,* and *Untitled.*

McGuinn managed to keep the Byrds franchise going until 1973; the original lineup reconvened for a disappointing one-shot reunion LP that demonstrated how the innovative style the band had pioneered wound up devolving into the tame California soft-rock of the 1970s. Still, various ex-Byrds remained prominent citizens in the rock community: Crosby pursued his variation on harmony-based folk-rock with Crosby, Stills and Nash (in later years, Canadian singer-songwriter Neil Young performed and recorded with CSN on an on-again, off-again basis). Gene Clark emerged as a consistently rewarding if not particularly prolific solo artist. The year 1979 saw McGuinn, Clark, and Hillman attempt a moderately successful but short-lived recording alliance. Hillman achieved country stardom in the late eighties as leader of the Desert Rose Band, while McGuinn emerged from a decade-long recording hiatus with 1991's *Back from Rio.*

Gram Parsons died of a drug overdose in 1973. Clarence White was killed by a drunk driver in 1973; Gene Clark died in 1991; and Michael Clarke died two years later. Strangely, the deaths of original members Clark and Clarke came shortly after the two had been excluded from a handful of low-key reunion projects. McGuinn, Crosby, and Hillman had played Byrds sets at a pair of benefit shows in L.A., in an attempt to establish a legal claim to the band name, which Clark and Clarke had appropriated for touring purposes in the eighties. The short-lived reunion also yielded four new studio tracks that were included on a 1990 Byrds retrospective boxed set.

The final Byrds lineup, featuring renowned bluegrass picker Clarence White (left) and sole charter member Roger McGuinn (right), blended acid rock with a country twang.

Love's original lineup—from left to right, Bryan MacLean, John Echols, Arthur Lee, Ken Forssi, and Alban "Snoopy" Pfisterer—combined a punklike urgency with folk-rock jangle.

LOVE

Although their L.A. contemporaries (and Elektra Records labelmates) the Doors ultimately became bigger stars, it was the seminal folk-punk-psychedelic combo Love, led by eccentric visionary Arthur Lee (b. 1944), who perhaps best embodied the early Sunset Strip rock scene. The band never fared particularly well commercially—thanks in part to Lee's vaunted contrariness and aversion to touring—but Love's best work has stood the test of time to influence a variety of bands.

The Memphis-born Lee had been knocking around in local combos since the early sixties. He formed the original Love with fellow singer-guitarist (and former Byrds roadie) Bryan MacLean (b. 1947) in 1965; the band was originally known as the Grassroots, but Lee had to change the name when another soon-to-be-famous L.A. act adopted it. Offering a harder, more aggressive variation on the Byrds' jangly style, Love's self-titled 1966 debut album spawned a pop hit in a pulsating cover of Burt Bacharach and Hal David's "My Little Red Book." Love's second album, *Da Capo*—for which Lee added horns, keyboards, and openly drug-influenced lyrics—featured the apocalyptic garage-punk standard "Seven and Seven Is," along with one of rock's first-ever side-long cuts, the nineteen-minute-long "Revelation."

But Love's psychedelic tendencies bloomed more satisfyingly on the 1968 magnum opus *Forever Changes*, which many have cited as an American equivalent of *Sgt. Pepper's Lonely Hearts Club Band*. Ambitiously constructed songs like "Along Again Or," "You Set the Scene," and "A House Is Not a Motel" sported inventive string and horn arrangements, expansive melodies, and intoxicatingly trippy lyrics that have earned the album its status as an underground classic.

But growing instability—both within the band and within Lee's consciousness—kept Love from recapturing the dizzy heights of *Forever Changes*. The next Love album, 1969's *Four Sail*, found Lee fronting a new set of musicians and delivering a rougher, stripped-down version of the prior lineup's style. The subsequent releases *Out Here* (1969) and *False Start* (1970) were spotty affairs boasting scattered moments of brilliance but generally lacking the lyrical twists and melodic subtleties that distinguished prior Love efforts; the latter disc featured one track from Lee's otherwise-unreleased collaboration with Jimi Hendrix, *The Everlasting First*.

Following the bizarre 1972 solo effort *Vindicator* and 1974's unsatisfying *Reel to Real* (featuring another new version of Love), Arthur Lee largely lived the life of a cult casualty, emerging for occasional L.A. club gigs and infrequent low-profile record releases. In the nineties, Lee finally began touring regularly, maintaining separate backing bands—all bearing the name Love—in L.A., New York, and England.

Arthur Lee (third from left) leads a late-sixties Love lineup. He would subsequently use the name for a series of bands, and continues to do so in the nineties.

THE DOORS

If the rise of psychedelic rock offered artists and listeners an array of new and more extreme sounds, it also opened up new lyrical and conceptual horizons. No sixties band explored the new music's literary potential more provocatively than the Doors. Frontman Jim Morrison (1943–1971) combined slithery sexual charisma with an apocalyptic lyrical vision whose images of violence and dread pointedly undercut the hippie culture's more romantic notions; the group's instrumental axis—keyboardist Ray Manzarek (b. 1935), guitarist Robby Krieger (b. 1946), and drummer John Densmore (b. 1945)—brought Morrison's lyrical visions to disturbing life. The Doors explored the dark underside of the Summer of Love, generating a memorable body of work that remains popular a quarter century after the band's breakup.

The Doors' highbrow leanings were established early in the band's history. According to legend, fellow ex-UCLA-film-students-turned-acid-experimenters Morrison and Manzarek hatched the band's concept during a chance meeting on Venice Beach, after aspiring poet Morrison read Manzarek his poem "Moonlight Drive." With Krieger and Densmore completing the lineup (in the absence of a bassist, Manzarek provided the bass lines on keyboards), the band—named by Morrison in honor of Aldous Huxley's book *The Doors of Perception*—soon became a familiar presence on the Hollywood club scene. By the summer of 1966, they'd scored a gig as house band at the Whisky A Go Go, but were fired after four months—reportedly due to the Oedipal outbursts of Morrison's epic mini-opera, "The End."

Jim Morrison, shown here at a New York City show in 1968, embodied the psychedelic ideal of sensory exploration.

Some early interest from Columbia Records led to a short-term development deal that yielded little of substance other than some instrumental gear—including a Vox organ that Manzarek began playing onstage instead of piano and that quickly became an integral element of the band's sound. By the time Elektra president Jac Holtzman had signed the Doors to his label, Morrison's lyrical vision had grown darker and more distinctive, as had the sound of the band's music.

The Doors' eponymous 1967 debut album wasn't an immediate success, and the first single chosen by Elektra—the bluntly aggressive "Break On Through," which merged images of chaos with a yearn-

The rock star as shaman: Jim Morrison strikes a typically pensive onstage pose.

ing for spiritual transcendence—flopped commercially. But the label persisted, and a second single—an edited version of the seven-minute, Krieger-written "Light My Fire"—became a boundary-shattering smash, bridging AM pop radio and the still-emerging FM progressive format. But the real evidence of the quartet's audaciousness was in the eleven-and-a-half-minute opus "The End," whose hauntingly morbid images of love, violence, guilt, and death made it clear that the Doors had a considerably more challenging agenda than did most of their counterculture contemporaries.

The group's equally impressive second and third albums, *Strange Days* (featuring appealing yet disturbing tunes like "People Are Strange," "Love Me Two Times," and "When the Music's Over") and *Waiting for the Sun* (including such similarly menacing numbers as "Hello, I Love You" and "Five to One"), enhanced the group's reputation and maintained its commercial ascendancy. But Morrison's increasingly self-destructive, alcohol-fueled behavior was beginning to drain the Doors' momentum.

The singer's self-mythologizing drunken-outlaw-poet image (reflected in his poem "The Celebration of the Lizard King," printed as part of the cover art on

Waiting for the Sun) was bolstered by a series of arrests: first on a public obscenity charge at a New Haven, Connecticut, concert in December 1967; for disorderly conduct on an airplane in August 1968; and, most famously, for allegedly exposing himself onstage at a March 1969 show in Miami. Although the 1969 charges were eventually dropped, that incident seriously sidetracked the band, with court proceedings keeping Morrison in Miami for much of 1969.

By that point, Morrison's interest in the Doors seemed to have been diverted into other projects. The band's 1969 album, *The Soft Parade* (whose Krieger-penned pop hit "Touch Me" was noticeably lacking in the irony that had lent a subversive tinge to the success of "Light My Fire"), suffered from slick, cluttered production, and it ultimately disappointed hard-core fans. Morrison, meanwhile, directed a film, *A Feast of Friends,* and wrote two books, *An American Prayer* and *The Lords and the New Creatures.*

The Doors bounced back somewhat with a pair of more cohesive albums, 1970's *Morrison Hotel* (including the fiercely rocking "Roadhouse Blues" and the haunting "Waiting for the Sun") and the following year's *L.A. Woman* (spotlighting the doomy radio favorites "L.A. Woman," "Love Her Madly," and "Riders on the Storm"). Both discs saw the group recovering some of its earlier focus and sharpening its musical attack, but Morrison's lyrics

betrayed an air of resignation, as if his original defiance had been eaten away by his legal problems and his over-indulgences. Shortly after *L.A. Woman* was completed, Morrison took a leave of absence from the band and moved with his wife, Pamela, to Paris, where he wrote and boozed until dying of heart failure in his bathtub on July 3, 1971, at the age of twenty-seven.

Manzarek, Krieger, and Densmore subsequently recorded two mostly ignored albums, *Other Voices* (1971) and *Full Circle* (1972), and reunited in 1978 for the album *An American Prayer,* which matched their new instrumental pieces with previously unreleased spoken-word performances by Morrison.

Morrison's Paris grave quickly became a magnet for fans bearing gifts, flowers, and graffiti pens.

In 1967, Jim Morrison was clearly a new breed of rock star: thoughtful, intense, and overtly sexual. His stage persona would continue to influence rock performers for decades to come.

Morrison has become even more popular as a dead icon than he was as a live rock star. The continuing growth of the Morrison cult of personality is reflected in the Doors' continuing prominence on classic-rock radio playlists and the success of director Oliver Stone's highly romanticized 1991 film *The Doors*, in which Val Kilmer portrayed Morrison as a wide-eyed psychedelic pilgrim. Further, Morrison's rocker-as-shaman stance has lived on in front men from Iggy Pop (who at one point was considered by the surviving Doors as a replacement for Morrison) to Axl Rose.

SPIRIT

The Los Angeles quintet Spirit was one of the stranger bands to emerge from the psychedelic era's embrace of oddball eclecticism. While the group never achieved more than moderate commercial success, the fact that Spirit's mix of hard-rock, blues, folk, and jazz influences could achieve any sort of mainstream recognition says a lot about the open-mindedness engendered by the vibe of the times.

Spirit's fundamental quirkiness was deeply ingrained. Shaven-headed drummer Ed Cassidy (b. 1931) had played with the likes of Thelonious Monk, Art Pepper, Cannonball Adderley, and Gerry Mulligan in the fifties before forming his own New Jazz Trio (which included future Spirit keyboardist John Locke [b. 1943]) and playing in an early version of Taj Mahal and Ry Cooder's legendary folk-blues-rock combo, the Rising Sons, during the sixties. In 1965, Cassidy began sitting in with fourteen-year-old guitarist Randy Wolfe's (b. 1951) band the Red Roosters, which included future Spirit members Jay Ferguson (b. 1947) and Mark Andes (b. 1948).

The Red Roosters broke up the following year when Cassidy—who had married Wolfe's mother—moved his new family to New York. There, Randy Wolfe met Jimi Hendrix (who was then calling himself Jimmy James) and joined Hendrix's band the Blue Flames; it was supposedly Hendrix who gave Wolfe his new stage name, Randy California. The following year, California and Cassidy returned to L.A. and ran into Ferguson and Andes at a love-in at Griffith Park; soon after, the Red Roosters reformed as Spirits

The original Spirit, from left to right: Randy California, Ed Cassidy, Mark Andes, John Locke, and Jay Ferguson.

Though less of a household name than Hendrix, Garcia, or Clapton, Spirit guitarist Randy California was one of the psychedelic era's most inventive axmen.

Rebellious (after Kahlil Gibran's book of the same name) with the addition of keyboardist John Locke, who claimed to be a direct descendant of the English philosopher of the same name.

The group—which soon shortened its name to Spirit—quickly earned a local reputation with live performances that featured extended, jazz-informed improvisations. In August 1967, two months after Spirit performed at the Monterey Pop Festival, record producer and event co-organizer Lou Adler signed the band to his Ode label. Adler produced the band's eponymous debut album, which appeared in January 1968 and included such eccentrically inventive tunes as "Fresh Garbage," "Mechanical World," and the instrumental "Taurus," whose opening section was later blatantly echoed in Led Zeppelin's "Stairway to Heaven." Though the LP softened the band's rawer edges somewhat, it nonetheless captured a good deal of Spirit's inventiveness.

The fivesome's sophomore release, *The Family That Plays Together,* followed in the autumn of 1968 and yielded Spirit's biggest single, California's "I Got a Line on You," which made it as high as number twenty-five. *Clear,* released in the summer of 1969, was a commercial and musical disappointment, but the subsequent non-album single "1984" was considerably more impressive and seemed like a natural follow-up hit. Unfortunately, the majestic tune's lyrical content, which equated the L.A. police department's riot-control methods with those of George Orwell's totalitarian Big Brother, limited the song's exposure on Top 40 stations.

For 1967's *The Twelve Dreams of Dr. Sardonicus,* Spirit moved from Ode to the larger Epic label and worked with new producer David Briggs. The album, which included such inventive numbers as "Nature's Way," "Mr. Skin," and "Prelude/Nothing to Hide," was the band's most ambitious and accomplished effort to date. Though it's since been acclaimed as the band's masterwork, at the time it failed to chart any higher than number sixty-three. Meanwhile, the group was splitting into factions, with California, Cassidy, and Locke wanting to continue exploring new musical horizons, and Ferguson and Andes leaning in a more commercial-rock direction.

In June 1971, Ferguson and Andes left Spirit to form the straight-ahead rock foursome Jo Jo Gunne. California, Cassidy, and Locke chose to soldier on, recruiting Texas-born brothers Al and Chris Staehely as replacements. But California soon dropped out; Cassidy, Locke, and the Staehely brothers recorded a new album, *Feedback,* released in early 1972. Though the disc bore the Spirit name, Al Staehely's tiresome macho rock songs showed none of the original band's imagination. Cassidy and Locke soon called it quits, leaving the two hapless newcomers to assemble their own version of Spirit to tour behind the album.

California reemerged as a pseudonymous soloist with the 1972 album *Kaptain Kopter and the Fabulous Twirly Birds,* which featured Cassidy (a.k.a. Cass Strange) on drums. California and Cassidy toured with bassist Larry Knight as a trio and began recording a cartoonishly conceptual follow-up, *The Adventures of Kaptain Kopter and Commander Cassidy in Potatoland,* which wouldn't be released until 1980. The trio re-adopted the name Spirit for a European tour, after which California temporarily quit the business and retreated to Hawaii, while Cassidy—always the group's most visually identifiable member—put together yet another tenuously derived Spirit to perform the band's old material.

California returned to active musical duty in 1974, and in the years since, he and Cassidy have kept the Spirit name active, touring regularly and recording albums for a variety of labels. Locke, who became a member of the Scottish hard-rock band Nazareth in 1968, and Andes, who joined soft-rockers Firefall in the late seventies and medium-hard coed rockers Heart in the eighties, have been occasional participants in some of those projects. Ferguson even completed the original lineup for the 1984 album *The Spirit of '84* (titled *The*

Thirteenth Dream overseas). Unfortunately, that reunion effort consisted mostly of redundant re-recordings of the band's best-known songs. California and Cassidy, now into his seventies, have continued to tour and record as Spirit.

Though the original Spirit splintered in 1971, Randy California (left) and Ed Cassidy (right) have kept the band name active.

The "In-A-Gadda-Da-Vida" vintage Iron Butterfly, left to right: Erik Braunn, Doug Ingle, Lee Dorman, and Ron Bushy.

IRON BUTTERFLY

These days, Iron Butterfly's lugubrious 1968 magnum opus "In-A-Gadda-Da-Vida" is viewed derisively as a dated relic, a quaint one-stop sampler of the most ham-handed excesses of the late-sixties rock. Indeed, with its murky, quasimystical lyrics, impenetrable wall-of-mud sound, and interminable drum solo, the seventeen-and-a-half-minute track, which occupied the entire second side of the band's second LP, would seem to contain virtually every psychedelic cliché imaginable. But at the time of its release, the song—whose title, according to its author, keyboardist-vocalist Doug Ingle (b. 1946), is hippie pig-Latin for "in the garden of Eden"—represented the cutting edge of the new "progressive" rock.

The Iron Butterfly that made "In-A-Gadda-Da-Vida" was actually the band's second recording incarnation. The original lineup—Ingle, singer Darryl DeLoach, guitarist Danny Weis, bassist Jerry Penrod, and drummer Ron Bushy (b. 1945)—formed in San Diego in 1966, later moved to Los Angeles, became a fixture on that city's booming club scene, and released a debut album early in 1968—the appropriately monikered underground hit *Heavy*.

Tours with the Doors and Jefferson Airplane helped keep *Heavy* on the charts for nearly a year, but it wasn't long before internal struggles resulted in DeLoach, Weis, and Penrod departing the band. The latter pair became founding members of Rhinoceros, which possessed the dubious distinction of being one of the first manufactured rock supergroups. Ingle, meanwhile, took control of Iron Butterfly's lead-vocal slot and conceptual reins, recruiting bassist Lee Dorman (b. 1945) and eighteen-year-old guitar prodigy Erik Braunn (b. 1950) to form the band featured on *In-A-Gadda-Da-Vida*, which hit the record-store racks before the year was out.

Despite its back-to-the-garden references, "In-A-Gadda-Da-Vida" (written, according to Ingle, during an acid trip) possessed a crudely menacing sonic ambience that contrasted sharply with its idyllic lyrics. The album quickly became Atlantic Records's biggest-selling album (until Led Zeppelin came along a year later), spending a whopping 140 weeks on the charts and more than a year and a half in the Top Ten, while a drastically edited version of the song made it to number thirty on the singles charts.

Though its use of volume and distortion presaged the emergence of heavy metal, much of the song's historical significance lies in its sheer length. FM album-rock radio was still in its infancy, and the song tested the new format's limits, helping to open the airwaves to longer pieces. The song also provided the nightly climax to the band's live shows, accompanied by such characteristically over-the-top touches as an onstage altar complete with burning pyres.

In-A-Gadda-Da-Vida's success made major stars of Iron Butterfly, and their subsequent releases *Ball* (1969) and *Live* (1970) kept the band on the charts even if they fell short of their predecessor's monstrous sales figures. But the foursome was ultimately torn apart by a combination of tax problems and ego battles between Ingle and Braunn, whose Machiavellian struggles frequently manifested themselves onstage. Braunn left and the band replaced him with a pair of axmen, Mike Pinera (b. 1948) and Larry "Rhino" Reinhardt (b. 1948), for the 1971 album *Evolution/Metamorphosis*, before splitting up entirely. Three years later, Braunn (who in the interim had discovered white-trash southern rockers Black Oak Arkansas, as well as forming Flintwhistle with early Butterfly members Penrod and DeLoach) and Bushy exhumed the Iron Butterfly name for two largely ignored albums. Since the late eighties, various combinations of band alumni have toured under the Iron Butterfly banner.

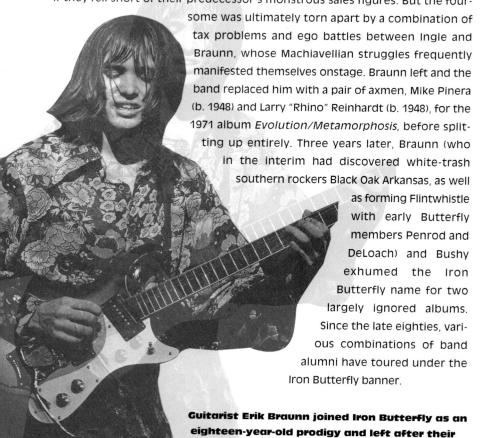

Guitarist Erik Braunn joined Iron Butterfly as an eighteen-year-old prodigy and left after their disappointing live album was released in 1970.

STEPPENWOLF

Unlike many of the bands that emerged in the wake of hippie rock's first wave, Steppenwolf possessed solid rock 'n' roll chops honed by its core members' years of experience as hardworking bar-band pros. But Steppenwolf also possessed a genuine affinity for the psychedelic movement's bohemian and political ideals, and created memorable music by blending acid rock's sense of adventure with a direct, no-nonsense musical attack. Though Steppenwolf's hard-edged anthems possessed a sense of righteous anger that was far removed from flower power, the band—led by legally blind front man John Kay (b. 1944, né Joachim Krauledat), who was rarely seen without his shades—shared the hippie movement's rebellious ideals.

Though Steppenwolf formed in Los Angeles in 1967, the group's roots stretch back to the early sixties in Toronto. It was there that Kay—who had es-

The savage young Steppenwolf in its prime. Front man John Kay, rarely seen without sunglasses, is second from left.

caped with his mother from his native East Germany as a child—fronted Sparrow, a locally popular blues-rock band. After a brief relocation to New York, Sparrow moved to Los Angeles, where they soon broke up. But the interest of ABC Records' staff producer Gabriel Mekler convinced Kay to reenlist Sparrow members Goldy McJohn (b. 1945) (keyboards) and Jerry Edmonton (b. 1946) (drums), and add Americans Michael Monarch (b. 1950) (guitar) and Ruston Moreve (b. 1948) (bass) to form a new group which Mekler christened Steppenwolf, after Hermann Hesse's mystical novel.

From Steppenwolf's 1968 debut onward, the band was well received by Top 40 and progressive radio, both of which embraced hard-charging hits like "Born to Be Wild" (written by former Sparrow guitarist Dennis Edmonton [b. 1946], who'd rechristened himself Mars Bonfire), "Magic Carpet Ride," and "Rock Me." These and other Steppenwolf tunes invoked psychedelic imagery

and hippie rhetoric while spotlighting Kay's insistent vocals and the band's pulsating guitar/organ interplay.

Steppenwolf's aggressive sound and leather-clad look often got them tagged as a biker band, and indeed they maintained a loyal following among motorcyclists. But they also possessed a stubborn activist streak that manifested itself in the group's willingness to endanger their underground credibility by covering Hoyt Axton's antidrug song "The Pusher." The band's iconoclastic politics were perhaps best represented by their 1969 protest hit "Monster," a thoughtful plea for mainstream America to recognize the peace movement's spiritual ties to traditional American ideals. At one point, Kay even ran for a seat on the Los Angeles City Council.

Steppenwolf's long-term influence extended beyond the band's own music. In addition to helping to popularize the fundamentals of what would soon

become hard rock, they were also the first to actually use the term "heavy metal," which pops up in the lyrics of "Born to Be Wild."

The band announced its breakup with the 1972 album *Rest in Peace;* by that time Monarch had been succeeded by Larry Byrom (b. 1948) and later Kent Henry, and Moreve by ex–Sparrow member Nick St. Nicholas (b. 1943), who in turn was replaced by George Biondo (b. 1945). Kay launched a mostly unsuccessful solo career before reviving Steppenwolf for three more albums, after which he returned to solo work.

Though it might have seemed that Steppenwolf had outlived its usefulness, the band—or at least its name and image—was good for one more comeback. In 1980, Kay and Jerry Edmonton, angry that McJohn and St. Nicholas had appropriated the Steppenwolf tag for low-rent live gigs, regained legal rights to the name. Kay hit the road again with an entirely new Steppenwolf lineup, which continues to tour and record into the nineties.

In the 1980s, John Kay (left) bounced back, fronting an all-new Steppenwolf lineup, achieving success as a touring act while recording only sporadically.

THE CHAMBERS BROTHERS

During the psychedelic era, only a handful of black artists—Jimi Hendrix, Rich Havens, Sly and the Family Stone, Arthur Lee—were consistently embraced young white rock audiences. Among these artists were the Chambers Brother an anomaly on the late-sixties rock scene not only because they were black, b also because they came from a gospel background and were considerably old than the white rock fans who helped make the Top Ten "Time Has Come Toda an AM/FM crossover smash in 1968. At that time, brothers George (b. 1931), Wil (b. 1938), Lester (b. 1940), and Joe (b. 1942) ranged in age from twenty-six to thir seven, and had been performing together professionally for seven years.

The four brothers, who grew up in a poor Mississippi sharecropping fam and got their musical start singing in church, drifted to Los Angeles in the early s ties and began performing as an acoustic folk-blues-gospel quartet, before addi white drummer Brian Keenan (b. 1944) and experimenting with amplified volun and fuzz pedals. Their hard-soul style, presaging what would come to be known funk, was popular in both psychedelic ballrooms and the more traditional bla R&B venues. Though the Chambers Brothers never produced another track memorable or successful as "Time Has Come Today," that tumultuous tune effo lessly encapsulates the mix of fear and exhiliration that typified the era.

Graduating from the folk-blues circuit to psychedelic ballrooms, The Chambers Brothers enjoyed a brief vogue with rock audiences, thanks to the trenchant hit "Time Has Come Today."

Despite the lasting appeal of their sole hit, "Incense and Peppermints," relatively little is known about The Strawberry Alarm Clock's history.

THE STRAWBERRY ALARM CLOCK

The Strawberry Alarm Clock's goofily irresistible 1967 number one hit, "Incense and Peppermints," illustrates how far the psychedelic revolution—or at least a sanitized version of it—penetrated the mainstream pop industry. The song, written by producers Tim Gilbert and John Carter, was the brainchild of studio professionals rather than hippie bohemians. However dubious its pedigree, though, the song effortlessly combined a propulsive melody, airy harmonies, and a panoply of flower-power slogans to create one of the era's catchiest singles.

The band that performed as The Strawberry Alarm Clock, including guitarist Ed King, who in the seventies would become a founding member of southern-rock giants Lynyrd Skynyrd, was a sextet from Santa Barbara. But "Incense and Peppermints" bore little resemblance to such ersatz band-written originals as "Strawberries Mean Love," "Birdman of Alkatrash," and "Sit with the Guru" that dominated the group's albums, leading many to surmise that the hit was the work of studio players. A Strawberry Alarm Clock reunion was attempted in the eighties, but did nothing to alter the band's one-hit-wonder status.

Though "Incense and Peppermints" is probably the most successful example of prefab psychedelia, it's hardly the only one. Others would include 1967's "The Shape of Things to Come," written by Tin Pan Alley vets Barry Mann and Cynthia Weil and credited to Max Frost and the Troopers (a.k.a. the fictional-rock-star-turned-president played by Christopher Jones in the campy teen-rebellion flick *Wild in the Streets*), and Kenny Rogers and the First Edition's 1968 attempt at stoned profundity, "Just Dropped in (To See What Condition My Condition Was In)." On these songs and others like them, issues of "authenticity" are rendered moot by the fact that these professionally constructed replicas of psychedelia have withstood the passage of time more gracefully than many of the era's more "genuine" efforts.

THE 13TH FLOOR ELEVATORS

Even before Buddy Holly changed the face of white rock 'n' roll in the 1950s, the state of Texas—despite its history of political conservatism—had long been a hotbed of musical independence, spawning such influential nonconformists as Bob Wills, T-Bone Walker, and Ornette Coleman. In the sixties, the Lone Star state produced such significant rock 'n' roll individualists as Doug Sahm, Bobby Fuller, and Sam the Sham, alongside such lesser-known but notable garage-rockers as Kenny and the Kasuals, and Mouse and the Traps. It shouldn't be surprising, then, that Texas was host to one of the first psychedelic music scenes; nor should it be surprising that the edgily eccentric, defiantly weird bands spawned there never found the commercial acceptance attained by many of their San Francisco and Los Angeles counterparts.

The 13th Floor Elevators—the first and greatest of the Texas psychedelic bands—are widely credited with inventing psychedelic music, and it is a claim that would be hard to dispute. Indeed, as early as 1965 the Elevators were already making an otherworldly racket that to many ears put their West Coast contemporaries to shame.

The Elevators started in Austin in 1965, when University of Texas student, self-styled guru, and avid LSD experimenter Tommy Hall decided to form a rock band to spread his homemade expanded-consciousness gospel. To bring his vision to life, Hall began by recruiting seventeen-year-old singer-guitarist Roky Erickson (b. 1947) from the Spades, a local band that had scored a regional hit with the Erickson composition "You're Gonna Miss Me." He then added guitarist Stacy Sutherland, bassist Benny Thurman, and drummer John Ike Walton from a local frat-rock group, the Lingsmen. Nonmusician Hall played an amplified "electric jug" that added to the band's instrumental dementia.

The intensity of the Elevators' live performances is as legendary as their prodigious ingestion of hallucinogenic drugs. Erickson's possessed, pleading vocals arched over his and Sutherland's feedback-laced guitars, while Hall's jug manically punctuated the backbeat provided by Walton (later replaced by Danny Thomas) and Thurman (who was succeeded by Ronnie Leatherman and then Danny Galindo). Fellow Texas misfit Janis Joplin had occasionally performed with the Elevators, and almost joined the group before she moved to San Francisco from Austin; those in the know claim that Erickson's singular howl was a key influence on Joplin's vocal style.

Lone Star lysergic kings the 13th Floor Elevators—left to right, Tommy Hall, Roky Erickson, Stacy Sutherland, John Ike Walton, and Ronnie Leatherman—are widely credited with inventing psychedelic rock.

The 13th Floor Elevators cut their first single in late 1965, a screaming remake of "You're Gonna Miss Me" initially released on the local Contact label. Lelan Rogers, brother of country music star Kenny Rogers, licensed the master and released the song nationally on his International Artists label, which had become something of a haven for eccentric regional acts like Bubble Puppy, who were best remembered for their 1969 hit "Hot Smoke and Sasafras." "You're Gonna Miss Me" rose to number fifty-six on the national charts, scoring the band TV appearances on relatively conservative teen dance shows, including *American Bandstand*. They followed the single with a brilliant debut album, *The Psychedelic Sounds of the 13th Floor Elevators*, on which songs like "Reverberation (Doubt)" and "Roller Coaster" boasted startlingly intense music and artfully convoluted, visionary lyrics inspired by Hall's acid mysticism. The album's title is generally cited as the first usage of the word "psychedelic" as a musical description.

The Elevators' progress was severely impeded by harrassment from local law-enforcement authorities, a situation which led to a temporary move to the more hospitable environs of San Francisco, where the band became a regular at such venues as the Fillmore and the Avalon Ballroom. After returning to Texas in early 1966, the seemingly inevitable drug bust occurred; although the musicians escaped with probation, police harrassment of the band escalated to the point where the musicians were regularly escorted to engagements by state troopers.

Following his release from a state mental hospital in 1972, former Elevators front man Roky Erickson carried his psychedelic influences to new extremes with a series of seminal solo recordings.

The band began to buckle under the pressure of the ongoing police persecution. Although the original rhythm section bailed out in 1967, Erickson, Sutherland, and Hall rallied to create a masterful second album, *Easter Everywhere*. But their two subsequent releases—the deceptively titled *Live*, which consisted of studio outtakes with unconvincingly overdubbed audience noise, and the disappointing studio effort *Bull of the Woods*—made it clear that the band's music was suffering under the strain.

The fatal blow was dealt in 1968, when Erickson and Sutherland were busted for marijuana possession. Sutherland was sentenced to Huntsville State Prison, while the increasingly idiosyncratic Erickson—who told the court of hearing voices and communicating with Martians—was offered the choice of going to prison or a mental hospital. He chose the latter, and was committed to Rusk State Hospital for the Criminally Insane (where he was diagnosed as schizophrenic) for three nightmarish years. Most observers agree that Erickson came out of the hospital with an even more tenuous grip on reality than when he entered. Upon his release in 1972, he and Walton attempted to assemble a new version of the Elevators, but the effort yielded only a few local performances.

Tommy Hall moved to California, where he still reportedly communicates with God on a regular basis. Stacy Sutherland was released from prison and was shot to death by his wife in 1978 during a domestic dispute. Roky Erickson eventually reemerged from obscurity to publicly declare himself a Martian and establish himself as a cult figure of the first order. Though the effects of his Elevators experiences had clearly taken a major toll on his psyche, Erickson's sporadic but seminal work in the seventies and eighties—commencing with the Doug Sahm–produced single "Red Temple Prayer (Two Headed Dog)"—showed him to be a harrowingly vital artist, carrying the inspiration of psychedelia to new levels of personal intensity, writing haunted songs dominated by demons, vampires, and aliens.

Erickson's work, both solo and with the Elevators, proved to be a crucial inspiration to more than one generation of free-thinking rockers. By 1990, he'd quit recording, fallen on hard times, and been institutionalized once again. Several admirers, including old Texas pals like Sahm and ZZ Top (whose guitarist Billy Gibbons had been a member of the Elevators-inspired Moving Sidewalks) and younger acts like R.E.M., The Jesus and Mary Chain, and Julian Cope (whose band the Teardrop Explodes had spearheaded a British psychedelic mini-revival in the early eighties), contributed interpretations of Roky's tunes to *Where the Pyramid Meets the Eye*, a tribute album that served both to raise money for the beleaguered artist and to remind a new generation of listeners of his and the Elevators' brilliance.

In 1995, the Austin-based independent label Trance Syndicate—run by King Coffey, whose band the Butthole Surfers has carried the Elevators' legacy of transcendent excess into the alternative rock era—released *All That May Do My Rhyme*, an album containing Roky's first new recordings in nearly a decade.

In recent years, Roky Erickson's unique post-Elevators rock has been embraced by a new generation of admirers.

DONOVAN

Donovan (b. 1946) is remembered largely for his rather self-conscious image as a mystical Aquarian-age minstrel, clad in flowing robes and drenched in patchouli. That this persona has often overshadowed his music is a shame, since beneath the kaftans and beads lies a very real and singular talent. Granted, during his hit-making heyday, Donovan did little to encourage the world to take him seriously, but the proof of his musical abilities lies in the grooves of the charmingly tuneful hits he released between 1966 and 1970.

The Scottish-born Donovan Leitch began his career as a blatantly Dylan-influenced message folkie, with early hits like "Catch the Wind" and "Colours." When protest music ran its course, Donovan relinquished his Dylan obsession

to adopt his more distinctive, though similarly naive, stance as a trippy troubadour. That approach yielded such baroque, acoustic-based hits as "Sunshine Superman," "Mellow Yellow," "Wear Your Love Like Heaven," "Barabajagal," "Hurdy Gurdy Man," "Jennifer Juniper," "Lalena," "Atlantis," and the atypically bluesy "Season of the Witch," all produced by English pop svengali Mickie Most and demonstrating a penchant for psychedelic lyrical allusions and a playful sense of tunesmanship.

Despite his enormous popularity, Donovan ultimately couldn't live up to his self-anointed poet-of-the-flower-people status. Many observers feel that the singer, who'd traveled with the Beatles to study meditation at Maharishi Mahesh Yogi's Indian retreat, severely damaged his counterculture credibility when he renounced drugs in favor of meditation.

Though his popularity faded toward the end of the decade, Donovan maintained his convictions. "The sixties were a party, a dream," he said in an interview during the 1980s. "We were discovering. We kept pushing the barriers to extremes, and that brought super success for socially concerned artists. . . . It became clear that the party was over in the seventies. We didn't sleep on the floor anymore, and the radical element asked, 'Am I going to continue to be radical, or should I be conservative and look after my house?'. . . I continued to live my ideals, but in obscurity."

Though Donovan kept a relatively low profile during the seventies and eighties, he continued to record and tour. By the nineties, it was starting to look as if Donovan and the world might be in sync again. In 1995, hipster entrepeneur Rick Rubin signed the artist to his American Recordings label, and the two began work on a new Donovan album.

As one of the most reliable hit-makers of the late sixties, Donovan brought the acceptable face of the psychedelic revolution to mainstream pop audiences.

TRAFFIC

If there was another psychedelic scene whose creative vitality could rival that of San Francisco, it was in London, where, just as they had during the original British Invasion, bands were refashioning American R&B and rock 'n' roll into something distinctly new. Even by 1967, relatively few American psychedelic records had been released in the United Kingdom, which left English musicians such as converted mods the Small Faces, colorful pop experimentalists the Move, and pixieish T. Rex leader Marc Bolan to use their imaginations to construct visions of their own.

At least in its initial incarnation, Traffic personified the sweetly skewed, listener-friendly approach of psychedelia's early British wing, presenting an organic melting pot of pop, folk, R&B, jazz, and ethnic influences. Through its checkered career, Traffic maintained an unmistakably sixties obliviousness to commercial concerns (indeed, the band's numerous breakups invariably occurred at the least opportune career junctures) while moving toward a more self-consciously jazz-oriented sound in the seventies.

Traffic's most prominent creative force was singer/multi-instrumentalist Stevie Winwood (b. 1948), who as a blues-wailing teen prodigy with the Spencer Davis Group had tasted pop success with the hits "Gimme Some Lovin'," "I'm a Man," and "Keep on Running." In 1967, frustrated with the band's stylistic limitations, the eighteen-year-old Winwood quit to explore new musical options, forming Traffic with guitarist-vocalist Dave Mason (b. 1947), drummer-lyricist Jim Capaldi (b. 1944), and saxophonist-flutist Chris Wood (b. 1944).

Steve Winwood learned to play guitar at a very young age and at the age of eight was a member, alongside his brother and father, of The Ron Atkinson Band.

Traffic in its first and most vital incarnation, left to right: Dave Mason, Steve Winwood, Chris Wood, and Jim Capaldi.

Less than three weeks after his final Spencer Davis gig, Winwood was in the studio with the other members of Traffic and producer Jimmy Miller to record the band's debut single, "Paper Sun," a timely confection whose sitar lines, Eastern percussion, and gently surrealistic lyrics perfectly captured the period's giddy innocence. It was an instant smash in Britain. Rather than move quickly to cash in on the song's success, the band spent six months getting its act together in a cottage in rural Berkshire Downs, writing, playing, tripping, and generally honing Traffic's musical identity. This period of the band's history would subsequently be romanticized by fans and journalists, but Winwood would later shatter that bucolic image by dismissing the scene as "four blokes not even out of their teens, shoved together and living in squalor."

Nonetheless, the rustic looseness of the communal living arrangement was reflected in the un-self-conscious exoticism of the band's landmark debut LP, *Mr. Fantasy*, which fit nicely into a pop scene energized by the revolutionary visions of *Sgt. Pepper's Lonely Hearts Club Band* and *Are You Experienced?*, thanks to such notable tunes as "Dear Mr. Fantasy," "Heaven Is in Your Mind," "Dealer," and the autobiographical "Berkshire Poppies."

By the time *Mr. Fantasy* was released in North America (with a new cover and a radically different track listing), Mason had quit the band; Traffic then toured as a trio. During a stop in New York on their return trip to England, they ran into Mason and patched things up, reenlisting their ex-bandmate in time for the sophomore LP, *Traffic*, an album as accomplished as its predecessor even if the songs' divergent styles—Mason's jauntily folksy

While playing with Traffic, Winwood pre-ferred to be unnoticeable behind large keyboards and equipment. However, as a solo-performer he took center stage, play-ing a portable keyboard.

"You Can All Join In" and Winwood's funk-driven "Pearly Queen"—hinted that the band was again on the verge of splintering.

Despite their ongo-ing popularity, Traffic split up in early 1969, leaving the patchy half-live, half-studio *Last Exit* as a less-than-stellar farewell. Wood and Capaldi briefly joined Mason and keyboardist Mick Weaver in an ill-fated alliance known as Mason, Capaldi, Wood and Frog. As for Winwood, an in-formal collaboration with Eric Clapton, himself fresh from the dissolution of his pioneering power-trio Cream, snowballed into Blind Faith, an overblown supergroup (also featuring for-mer Cream drummer Ginger Baker and ex–Family bassist Rick Grech) that yielded one mildly disappointing album and one disastrous tour.

After Blind Faith fell apart, Winwood began work on a solo project to be titled *Mad Shadows,* but he eventually called in old mates Capaldi and Wood; the album evolved into a new Traffic project. Released in 1970 as *John Barleycorn Must Die,* the new disc was hailed by many as the group's best. But the psychedelic el-ements of earlier Traffic efforts were less apparent in the music, which drew more than ever from Winwood's folk and jazz influences. The latter element would be-come increasingly pronounced on subsequent releases like the live *Welcome to the Canteen, The Low Spark of High-Heeled Boys,* and *Shootout at the Fantasy Factory,* all of which boasted expanded instrumental lineups and little of the band's original adventurousness. The introspective *When the Eagle Flies,* released in 1974, returned the band to a quartet format and a moodier feel, but Winwood's near-fatal bout with peritonitis soon afterward put the brakes on Traffic.

Mason and Capaldi recorded numerous solo albums in the seventies and eighties. Wood died in 1983 after a long illness. Winwood reemerged in the eighties as a mainstream solo star before attempting a Traffic reunion with Capaldi (with whom he'd frequently collaborated in the intervening years) and a new brace of sidemen on the 1994 album *Far from Home.*

The original, Syd Barrett-led Pink Floyd, left to right: Nick Mason, Barrett, Roger Waters, and Rick Wright.

PINK FLOYD

The version of Pink Floyd that in the 1990s routinely fills stadiums and racks up multiplatinum album sales bears little resemblance to the flamboyantly unconventional band that was pivotal to the launch of the British psychedelic movement of the sixties. Indeed, the massive commercial success that Pink Floyd achieved in the seventies was inconceivable in 1965, when the band's original leader, Syd Barrett (b. 1946)—a strikingly charismatic figure who would end up as one of the rock world's most tragic basket cases—first joined up with bassist Roger Waters (b. 1944), keyboardist Rick Wright (b. 1945), and drummer Nick Mason (b. 1945).

The group came into existence when singer-songwriter-guitarist Barrett, who was attending art school in London, joined architecture students Waters, Wright, and Mason in the aptly monikered band the Architectural Abdabs; Barrett soon rechristened the band the Pink Floyd Sound, combining the names of Georgia bluesmen Pink Anderson and Floyd Council. Though the group initially leaned toward American R&B and jazz, by 1967 the foursome had arrived at a more distinctive style, involving extended compositions and high-volume instrumental freak-outs alongside more delicate melodic textures and folk-blues elements. Pink Floyd was also one of the first English rock bands to test the limits of live presentation; their now-legendary shows at London's UFO Club were mind-bending multimedia events whose visual ingenuity was a perfect complement to the band's musical inventiveness.

In the studio, Barrett demonstrated a knack for gently eccentric, concisely trippy pop tunes, best demonstrated by the band's 1967 singles "See Emily Play" and "Arnold Layne," which both became Top 20 U.K. hits despite the fact that radio programmers balked at the latter song's lyrics about a neighborhood transvestite. But the dichotomy between the band's catchy pop numbers and their more volatile live identity caused problems when the group attempted to play outside London, where audiences knew only the hit singles. On a package tour of England with Jimi Hendrix, the Move, the Nice, and the Amen Corner, crowds reacted violently when the Floyd used its seventeen-minute nightly slot to play improvisational pieces rather than the familiar hits.

The year 1967 also saw the release of Pink Floyd's debut album, *The Piper at the Gates of Dawn,* which showcased the band's more experimental side on compelling extended pieces like "Interstellar Overdrive" and "Astronomy Domine." By the next year, however, Barrett's madness—allegedly due to his overindulgence in LSD—was clearly eclipsing his brilliance. With their increasingly erratic leader's involvement becoming questionable, the group brought in the even-tempered David Gilmour (b. 1944) to take up the slack on guitar and vocals.

By the time *A Saucerful of Secrets* appeared in 1968, Barrett had been ousted from the band. He appeared on only one *Saucerful* track, the frankly loopy "Jugband Blues," on which he sang, "I'm most obliged to you for making it clear/that I'm not really here." The rest of the album spotlighted such Waters compositions as the spacy title track and the drony "Set the Controls for the Heart of the Sun," both of which offered clues to Pink Floyd's future direction.

The increasingly unhinged Barrett managed to release two solo albums, *The Madcap Laughs* and *Barrett* (both 1970), with production and instrumental support from Gilmour, Waters, and Wright. Despite the artist's fragile mental state, both albums did a compelling job of capturing his skewed sensibility. Barrett would never record again, but fans often detected his shadowy influence in some of Pink Floyd's subsequent works, most notably their 1975 tribute "Shine on You Crazy Diamond."

One of rock's legendary mad geniuses, Roger "Syd" Barrett, is supposedly painting again.

After leaving Pink Floyd, Roger Waters oversaw an elaborate all-star restaging of *The Wall*, performed, appropriately enough, at the former site of the Berlin Wall.

Pink Floyd not only survived Barrett's departure but thrived in his absence, with Waters—whose sharp-edged misanthropy contrasted sharply with Barrett's addled whimsy—taking over most of his songwriting-conceptual duties, while Waters and Gilmour shared lead vocals. The band continued to pursue its art-rock muse in increasingly elaborate directions, both in their live shows and on albums like *More* (1969), *Ummagumma* (1969), *Atom Heart Mother* (1970), *Meddle* (1971), and *Obscured by Clouds* (1972).

When Pink Floyd finally hit mass-audience paydirt with 1973's *Dark Side of the Moon*, they did so with a vengeance. The album employed some of the most innovative uses of the recording studio to date, with inventive use of sound effects and synthesizers, along with such memorable compositions as "Money," "Breathe," "Us and Them," and "Brain Damage." The songs' lyrical themes of alienation and mental illness were assumed by many to allude to the plight of the band's fallen founder.

Dark Side of the Moon proved to be a monumental commercial success, permanently establishing Pink Floyd as one of rock's most consistently popular acts. In 1980, it became the longest consecutively charting album in music-business history, and remained on the charts for an incredible 741-week run that ended in October 1988. That success was all the more impressive in light of the group members' insistence on maintaining near-anonymity as individuals (their faces were never seen on album covers after *Meddle*).

Subsequent albums like *Wish You Were Here* (1975) and *Animals* (1977) mixed elaborately rendered soundscapes with Waters' bleak observations, while the band mounted increasingly elaborate stage productions that downplayed the musicians' presence in favor of projected film images and outsized props (a crash-

Bassist Roger Waters assumed Pink Floyd's conceptual reins after Syd Barrett's departure.

ing jet plane for the *Wish You Were Here* tour, an inflated flying pig for *Animals*). Though the seventies-model Floyd would receive considerable flak for Waters' lyrical cynicism, the songs' withering fatalism was in many respects a refreshingly humanistic alternative to the sterile self-importance that plagued the art-rock genre.

In 1979, the band unveiled Waters' magnum opus, *The Wall*, an expansive double LP built around a bitter, alienated rockstar character named Pink. The album, whose unlikely hit single "Another Brick in the Wall" was banned by numerous radio stations due to its supposed anti-education message, was accompanied by a stage show so elaborate that it could only be performed in New York, Los Angeles, and London. The concerts included a mock brick wall which was built onstage during the performances, eventually obscuring the band from the audience's view. In 1982, *The Wall* was made into a successful feature film, with Boomtown Rats lead singer Bob Geldof (b. 1954) in the lead role.

Despite *The Wall*'s multimedia success, it proved to be Floyd's last real collective effort, as acrimony escalated between Waters and his bandmates. The 1983 album *The Final Cut* was originally intended as a collection of the additional music featured in the film version of *The Wall*, but evolved into a freestanding conceptual work that was essentially a Waters solo effort.

The release of *The Pros and Cons of Hitchhiking*, Waters' 1984 solo album, was accompanied by Waters' announcement that Pink Floyd was finished, but his bandmates had other ideas. Despite Waters' threats of legal action, Gilmour, Mason, and Wright released the 1987 album *A Momentary Lapse of Reason* under the Pink Floyd banner. Though the album's pleasantly anonymous music suffered from the absence of Waters' trademark lyrical bite, the fans turned out in droves.

Since then, Roger Waters and the Gilmour-led Pink Floyd have continued to record and tour separately. Both have continued to mount elaborate concert extravaganzas, such as Waters's all-star 1990 restaging of *The Wall* at the site of the fallen Berlin Wall, and Pink Floyd's massive tour in support of its 1994 album, *The Division Bell*, which saw them playing in outdoor stadiums for ticket prices that frequently topped the hundred-dollar mark. Syd Barrett, meanwhile, continues to live quietly in his hometown of Cambridge, England.

CONCLUSION

In the three decades since the psychedelic muse first exercised its influence, psychedelia has remained a cornerstone in rock's foundation. Acts like the Doors, the Grateful Dead, and Jimi Hendrix, once considered the vanguard of rock's cutting edge, now represent the core of mainstream "classic rock." Meanwhile, the restless spirit of psychedelia continues to assert itself on a number of musical fronts.

While the musical and lifestyle-oriented lessons learned during the original acid-rock explosion have become subtly and deeply ingrained in the fabric of mainstream rock, they're more obviously apparent in various underground genres. An international underground of young bands melding a psychedelic influence with the raw energy of sixties-style garage rock continues to thrive. Meanwhile, more abrasive alternative-rock combos like the Butthole Surfers and the Flaming Lips continue to test the limits of rock's sonic extremes in a manner that echoes the experimentation of psychedelia's outer edge. Elsewhere, the hippie era's tribal ideals have been updated in the musical and social milieu of the dance-rave scene. House music, along with such stylistic offshoots as techno and ambient, meld psychedelia's adventurous, experimental spirit with state-of-the-art technology and multimedia communal performance-gatherings that echo the ballroom experiences of the late sixties in their emphasis on sensory saturation and, often, their participants' liberal use of illicit substances. And seemingly Grateful Dead–inspired, jam-oriented bands like the Spin Doctors, Blues Traveler, and Phish continue to maintain a massive following of young fans born long after the sixties faded.

The concept of "psychedelic music" long ago stopped referring strictly to music inspired by drugs. From a 1990s perspective, the term applies more broadly, to an attitude, a perspective, a desire for an alternate (and expanded) view of the universe—which is precisely the motivation that launched the psychedelic revolution in the first place.

The psychedelic music of the sixties opened up new means of expression and pointed the way for future bands to continue exploring musical boundaries.

SUGGESTED READING

Bangs, Lester. *Psychotic Reactions and Carburator Dung*. New York: Alfred A. Knopf, 1987.

Burdon, Eric. *I Used to Be an Animal, But I'm All Right Now*. Winchester, Mass. Faber and Faber, 1986.

DeCurtis, Anthony, James Henke, and Holly George-Warren. *The Rolling Stone Illustrated History of Rock 'n' Roll*. New York: Random House/Rolling Stone Press, 1992.

Heylin, Clinton. *Bob Dylan: Behind the Shades*. New York: Summit Books, 1991.

Kiersh, Edward. *Where Are You Now, Bo Diddley?* New York: Dolphin Books, 1986.

Kooper, Al, with Ben Edmonds. *Backstage Passes*. New York: Stein & Day, 1977.

Murray, Charles Shaar. *Crosstown Traffic: Jimi Hendrix and the Rock 'n' Roll Revolution*. New York: St. Martin's Press, 1990.

Norman, Philip. *Shout!: The Beatles in Their Generation*. New York: Fireside, 1981.

Rogan, John. *Timeless Flight: The Definitive Biography of the Byrds*. Chathom, N.Y.: Hallen Books, 1991.

Schaffner, Nicholas. *The Beatles Forever*. New York: McGraw-Hill, 1977.

———. *A Saucerful of Secrets: Pink Floyd Odyssey*. New York: Harmony Books, 1991.

Various. *The Rolling Stone Interviews 1967–1980*. New York: St. Martin's Press, 1981.

Various. *20 Years of Rolling Stone: What A Long Strange Trip It's Been*. New York: Friendly Press, 1987.

Ward, Ed, Geoffrey Stokes, and Ken Tucker. *Rock of Ages: The Rolling Stone History of Rock 'n' Roll*. New York: Summit, 1986.

SUGGESTED LISTENING

The Beatles, *Sgt. Pepper's Lonely Hearts Club Band*, Capitol

The Byrds, *Fifth Dimension*, Columbia

Country Joe and the Fish, *Electric Music for the Mind and Body*, Vanguard

Cream, *Disraeli Gears*, Polydor

Donovan, *Troubador: The Definitive Collection*, Epic/Legacy

The Doors, *The Doors*, Elektra

Bob Dylan, *Blonde on Blonde*, Columbia

The Grateful Dead, *Live Dead*, Warner Bros.

The Jimi Hendrix Experience, *Electric Ladyland*, MCA

The Incredible String Band, *The Hangman's Beautiful Daughter*, Hannibal

Iron Butterfly, *In-A-Gadda-Da-Vida*, Atco

Jefferson Airplane, *2400 Fulton Street*, RCA

Love, *Love Story: 1966–1972*, Rhino

Pink Floyd, *The Piper at the Gates of Dawn*, Capitol

Quicksilver Messenger Service, *Sons of Mercury: The Best of...*, Rhino

The Rolling Stones, *Their Satanic Majesties Request*, ABKCO

Alexander "Skip" Spence, *Oar*, Sony Music Special Products

Spirit, *Time Circle (1968–1972)*, Epic

Steppenwolf, *Born to Be Wild: A Retrospective*, MCA

The 13th Floor Elevators, *The Psychedelic Sounds of the 13th Floor Elevators*, Collectables

Traffic, *Smiling Phases*, Island

Various Artists, *Nuggets Volumes 1–3*, Rhino

Various Artists, *Pebbles Volumes 1–5*, Archive International

The Yardbirds, *The Yardbirds (Roger the Engineer)*, Edsel

PHOTOGRAPHY CREDITS

Cover Photography: © Adrian Boot/Retna: Pink Floyd; © Matthew McVay/ Tony Stone Images: peace symbol; © Michael Putland/ Retna: Steve Winwood; © Globe Photos: Iron Butterfly
© Archive Photos/ Russell Reif: p. 22–23
Courtesy Mrs. Evelyn Erickson: p. 46–47
© Globe Photos: p. 39; © Richard Polak: p. 53; © Jay Thompson: p. 59
Jason Laure: p. 7, 8 bottom
© Scott Newton: p. 48, 49
Michael Ochs Archive: p. 24–25, 30, 31, 36, 45
Photofeatures International: © Alec Byrne: p. 41; © Chris Walter: p. 27
Retna Ltd.: © Adrian Boot: p. 18, 55, 56, 57; © DeSoto: p. 38; © Jill Furmanowsky/ L. F. I.: p. 37; © Gary Gershoff: p. 58; © Beth Gwinn: p. 42; © Holland: p. 13; © King Collection: p. 12; © Michael Putland: p. 50, 52; © David Redfern: p. 10; © Anthony Stern: p. 35; © Ray Stevenson: p. 2
© Joseph Sia: p. 15, 17, 26, 28, 33, 40, 44, 54
Star File Photos: © Jim Cummings: p. 8 top; © Bob Gruen: p. 34; © Elliott Landy: p. 32; © Chuck Pulin: p. 19 bottom, 21
UPI/Bettman: p. 6, 9; © Amalie R. Rothschild: p. 16; © Springer Collection: p. 20

INDEX

Adler, Lou, 37
After Bathing at Baxter's (album), 21
Altamont Festival, 21
Amboy Dukes, 10
Amen Corner, 56, *56*
American Beauty (album), 18
An American Prayer (Morrison), 34
Anderson, Signe Toly, 20
Andes, Mark, 36, *36*, 38
Animals, 11
Anthem of the Sun (album), 18
Aoxomoxoa (album), 18
Aragon (Chicago), 8
Are You Experienced? (album), 13, 53
Avalon Ballroom (San Francisco), 8, 9, 17, 47
Axis: Bold As Love (album), 14
Axton, Hoyt, 43

Back from Rio (album), 29
Balin, Marty, 20, *20*, 21, 22, 23
Ball (album), 40
Ballad of Easy Rider (album), 29
Band of Gypsys, 14
Barbata, John, 22

Bark (album), 22
Baron Von Tollbooth and the Chrome Nun (album), 22
Barrett, Syd, 55, *55*, 56, *56*, 57, 58
Beach Boys, 11
Beatles, 11, *11*, 27, 51
Beefeaters, 28
Berry, Chuck, 12
Big Brother and the Holding Company, 9
Black Oak Arkansas, 40
Bless Its Pointed Little Head (album), 21
Blind Faith, 54
Blows Against the Empire (album), 22
Blue Flames, 12, 36
Blues for Allah (album), 18
Blues Traveler, 59
Bolan, Marc, 52
Boomtown Rats, 58
"Born to be Wild," 42, 43
Braunn, Erik, 39, *39*, 40, *40*
Briggs, David, 37
Bull of the Woods (album), 48
Burdon, Eric, 11
Bushy, Ron, 39, *39*, 40
Butthole Surfers, 49, 59
Byrds, 21, 27—29, *27, 28*
Byrom, Larry, 43

California, Randy, 36, *36, 37, 37*, 38, *38*
Calindo, Danny, 46
Capaldi, Jim, 52, *53*, 54
Carter, John, 45
Casady, Jack, 20, *20*, 22, 23
Cassidy, Ed, 36, *36*, 38, *38*
"The Celebration of the Lizard King" (Morrison), 33

Chambers Brothers, 44, *44*

Chaquico, Craig, 22

Cheetah (Los Angeles), 8

Cipollina, John, 24, 26

Clapton, Eric, 54

Clark, Gene, 27, *27*, 28, 29

Clarke, Michael, *27*, 28, 29

Cochran, Eddie, 12

Collins, Judy, 27

Cooder, Ry, 36

Costello, Elvis, 19

Country Joe and the Fish, 9

Cox, Billy, 14

Creach, Papa John, 22

Cream, 54

Crosby, David, 21, 22, 27–28, *27*, 29

Davis, Clive, 19

Deadheads, 16, 17

Deadicated (album), 19

Dead Set (album), 19

DeLoach, Darryl, 39, 40

Densmore, John, 32, 34

Desert Rose Band, 29

Dr. Byrds and Mr. Hyde (album), 29

Donovan, 10, 50–51, *50*

Doors, 10, 32–35, *32, 33, 34, 35*, 39, 59

The Doors (film), 35

Dorman, Lee, 39, *39*

Douglas, Alan, 15

Dragon Fly (album), 22

Drugs, 6, 7, 8, 9, 11, 13, 14, 17, 19, 24, 26, 32, 46, 47, 48, 51

Dryden, Spencer, 20, *20*

Duncan, Gary, 24, 26

Dylan, Bob, 10, 11, 14, 27, 28, 50

Easter Everywhere (album), 48

Echols, John, 30, *30*

Edmonton, Jerry, 42, 43

"Eight Miles High," 27, 28, 29

Electric Circus (New York), 8

The Electric Kool-Aid Acid Test (Wolfe), 7

Electric Ladyland (album), 14

Electric Sky Church, 14

Elmore, Greg, 24, 26

"The End," 32, 33

Erickson, Roky, 46, 48, *48, 49, 49*

Europe '72 (album), 18

The Everlasting First (album), 31

Evolution/Metamorphosis (album), 40

False Start (album), 31

The Family That Plays Together (album), 37

A Feast of Friends (film), 34

Feedback (album), 38

Ferguson, Jay, 36, *36*, 38

Fifth Dimension (album), 28

Fillmore (San Francisco), 8, 9, 17, 26, 47

Fillmore East (New York), 8, 14, *16*, 26, *26*

First Edition, 45

Flaming Lips, 59

Flying Burrito Brothers, 29

Forever Changes (album), 31

Forssi, Ken, 30, *30*

Four Sail (album), 31

Freedom at Point Zero (album), 23

Freiberg, David, 22, 24, 26

From the Mars Hotel (album), 18

Frost, Max, 45

Full Circle (album), 34

Fuller, Bobby, 46

Garcia, Jerry, 6, 16, *16*, 19, 22

Geldof, Bob, 58

Gibbons, Billy, 49

Gilbert, Tim, 45

"Gimme Some Lovin'," 52

Godchaux, Donna, 18, *18*

Godchaux, Keith, 18, *18*, 19

Graham, Bill, 9, *9*, 17, 26

Grateful Dead, 7, 9, 16–19, *16, 18, 19*, 59

Grateful Dead Live (album), 18

Great Society, 20, 21

Haight-Ashbury, 8, 9, 17, 20

Hall, Tommy, 46, *47*, 48, 49

Hammond, John Paul, 12

Hart, Mickey, 17

Havens, Richie, 44

"Hello, I Love You," 33

Helms, Chet, 9

Hendrix, Jimi, 12–15, *12, 13, 15*, 31, 36, 44, 56, *56*, 59

Henry, Kent, 43

Hillman, Chris, *27*, 28, 29

Holly, Buddy, 46

Hopkins, Nicky, 26

Hot Tuna, 22

"In-A-Gadda-Da-Vida," 39, 40

"Incense and Peppermints," 45

Ingle, Doug, 39, *39*, 40

In the Dark (album), 19

Iron Butterfly, 39–40, *39*

Isley Brothers, 12

James, Jimmy. *See*
  Hendrix, Jimi.
Jefferson Airplane, 9,
  10, 20–23, *20, 21, 22,
  23,* 39
"Jennifer Juniper," 51
Jet Set, 28
Jones, Christopher,
  45
Joplin, Janis, 8, *8,* 9, 46
Just For Love (album),
  26

Kantner, Paul, 20, *20,*
  21, 22, 23
*Kaptain Kopter and the
  Fabulous Twirly Birds*
  (album), 38
Kaukonen, Jorma, 20,
  20, 22, 23
Kaukonen, Peter, 22
Kay, John, 41, *41,* 42, *42,*
  43
KBC Band, 23
Keenan, Brian, 44
Kenny and the Kasuals,
  46
Kesey, Ken, *6,* 7, 17
Kilmer, Val, 35
King, B.B., 12
King, Ed, 45
King Curtis, 12
Knight, Curtis, 12
Kreiger, Robby, 32, 33,
  34
Kreutzmann, Bill, 17

Leary, Timothy, 7
Leatherman, Ronnie,
  46, *47*
Led Zeppelin, 40
Lee, Arthur, 30, *30,* 31,
  31, 44
Lesh, Phil, 16
"Light My Fire," 33, 34
Limelighters, 27
Lingsmen, 46
Little Richard, 12
Live (album), 40
Live/Dead (album), 18

Locke, John, 36, *36,* 37,
  38
Long John Silver
  (album), 22
*The Lords and the New
  Creatures* (Morrison),
  34
Love, 30–31, *30, 31*
Love and Spirit, 11
"Love Her Madly," 34
Lovett, Lyle, 19
Lynyrd Skynyrd, 45

MacLean, Bryan, 30, *30*
Mann, Barry, 45
Manzarek, Ray, 32, 33,
  34
Mason, Dave, 52, 53, *53,*
  54, 58
Mason, Nick, 55, *55*
McCartney, Paul, 13
McGuinn, Roger, 27, *27,*
  28
McJohn, Goldy, 42, 43
McKernan, Ron
  "Pigpen," 18
Mekier, Gabriel, 42
"Mellow Yellow," 51
Merry Pranksters, 7, 9,
  17
Midnight Lightning
  (album), 15
Midnight Oil, 19
Miles, Buddy, 14
Miller, Jimmy, 53
"Mr. Tambourine Man,"
  28
Mitchell, Chad, 27
Mitchell, Mitch, 12
Moby Grape, 20
Monterey Pop Festival,
  13, 17, *20,* 26, 37
Moreve, Ruston, 42
Morrison, Jim, 32, *32,*
  33, *33*
Morrison Hotel (album),
  34
Mouse and the Traps,
  46
Move, 52, 56, *56*

Murray, Jim, 24
Murray the K, 11
Mydland, Brent, 19

Nash, Graham, 29
Nazareth, 38
New Jazz Trio, 36
Nice, 56, *56*
Nine to the Universe
  (album), 15
"Nothing's Gonna Stop
  Us Now," 23
*The Notorious Byrd
  Brothers* (album), 29
Nugent, Ted, 10

Other Voices (album),
  34
Out Here (album), 31
Owsley, 9, 17

Parsons, Gram, 29
Peace by Piece (album),
  26
Penrod, Jerry, 39, 40
"People Are Strange,"
  33
Pet Sounds (album), 11
Pfisterer, Alban
  "Snoopy," 30, *30*
Phish, 59
Pickett, Wilson, 12
Pinera, Mike, 40
Pink Floyd, 55–58, *55*
Pop, Iggy, 35
Protests, 7, *7,* 8, 26, 43

Quicksilver Messenger
  Service, 9, 22, 24–26,
  24, 25, 26

Reckoning (album), 19
Red Octopus (album),
  23
Red Roosters, 36
Reel to Real (album), 31
R.E.M., 49
Rest in Peace (album),
  43
Rhinoceros, 39

INDEX

Rising Sons, 36
"Rock Me," 42
Rogers, Kenny, 45, 47
Rogers, Lelan, 47
"Roller Coaster," 47
Rolling Stones, 11, 22
Ron Atkinson Band, 52
Rose, Axl, 35
Rubin, Rick, 51

Sahm, Doug, 46, 49
St. Nicholas, Nick, 43
Sam the Sham, 46
Sears, Pete, 22
Seeger, Pete, 28
Sgt. Pepper's Lonely Hearts Club Band (album), 11, 31, 53
Shady Grove (album), 26
Shakedown Street (album), 19
"The Shape of Things to Come," 45
Slick, Grace, 20, *20*, 21, *21*, 22, 23
Sly and the Family Stone, 44
Small Faces, 52
Smile (album), 11
The Soft Parade (album), 34
"Somebody to Love," 21
Sparrow, 42
Spence, Alexander "Skip," 20
Spencer Davis Group, 52, 53
Spin Doctors, 59
Spirit, 36–38, *36, 37, 38*
The Spirit of '84 (album), 38
Spitfire and Earth (album), 23
Staehely, Al, 38
Staehely, Chris, 38

Stanley, Augustus Owsley, 9, 17
Steal Your Face (album), 18
Steppenwolf, 41–43, *41*
Stills, Stephen, 22, 29
Stone, Oliver, 35
Strange, Cass, 38
Strange Days (album), 33
Strawberry Alarm Clock, 45, *45*
"Summer of Love" (1967), 10, 17
Sunfighter (album), 22
"Sunshine Superman," 51
Surrealistic Pillow (album), 21
Sutherland, Stacy, 46, *47*, 48, 49
Sweetheart of the Rodeo (album), 29

Taj Mahal, 36
Tea Party (Boston), 8
Teardrop Explodes, 49
Terrapin Station (album), 19
Their Satanic Majesties Request (album), 11
The Thirteenth Dream (album), 38
13th Floor Elevators, 7, 46–49, *46*
Thirty Seconds Over Winterland (album), 22
Thomas, Danny, 46
Thomas, Mickey, 23
Thurman, Benny, 46
"Touch Me," 34
Traffic, 52–54
T. Rex, 52
Trips Festival, 9, 17
Troopers, 45
Turner, Ike and Tina, 12
"Turn! Turn! Turn!," 28
Turtles, 22

Untitled (album), 29

Valenti, Dino, 24, 26, *26*
Vega, Suzanne, 19
Vindicator (album), 31
Volunteers (album), 22

Waiting for the Sun (album), 33
Wake of the Flood, 18
The Wall (album), *57*, 58
Walton, John Ike, 46, *47*, 49
Waters, Muddy, 12
Waters, Roger, 55, *55*, 56, 57, 58, *58*
Weaver, Mick, 54
Weil, Cynthia, 45
Weir, Bob, 16, *19*
Weis, Danny, 39
What About Me (album), 26
Where the Pyramid Meets the Eye (album), 49
White, Clarence, 29
"White Rabbit," 21
"Who Do You Love," 26
Wild in the Streets (film), 45
Wills, Bob, 46
Wilson, Brian, 11
Wilson, Jackie, 12
Winwood, Steve, 52, *52*, 53, *53*, 54, *54*
Wolfe, Randy, 36
Wolfe, Tom, 7
Wood, Chris, 52, *53*, 54
Woodstock Festival, 14, 21
Workingman's Dead (album), 18
Wright, Rick, 55, *55*, 56

Young, Neil, 29
Younger Than Yesterday (album), 29

ZZ Top, 49